Management
for the
Christian
Leader

Management
for the
Christian
Leader

Olan Hendrix

Wayne Stayskal, *Illustrator*

A Mott Media Book

BAKER BOOK HOUSE
Grand Rapids, Michigan 49516

Formerly published under the title, *Management for the Christian Worker*
© 1976, 1981 by Baker Book House Company.

Paperback edition issued, August 1988

Library of Congress Catalog Card No. 76–3510
ISBN 0–8010–4337–9
Printed in the United States of America

To
Elizabeth

Contents

Foreword

Management is an inescapable part of living. Everyone is involved in management at one level or another. A person cannot wait until he or she is the head of an organization to learn about management. An individual living and working alone must manage time, money, talent, body, soul, and mind. The question about management is not whether you will manage, but whether you will manage well or poorly.

Most of us struggle with managing our lives, our businesses, or our ministries, realizing that we need to manage things better. We tend to blame circumstances rather than question our managerial skills when things turn out poorly.

Since management is a lifelong job on numerous levels, we can never rest on our laurels and think that we have mastered the job of managing. We must continually be refocusing, reading, studying, and learning more things to manage well in our ever-changing society.

I have known Olan Hendrix for over ten years. He has studied, practiced, and taught management. Olan is not an ivory-towered instructor with no practical experience. Neither is he a seat-of-the-pants pragmatician with no management theory. Olan is a student of management. Olan is a practitioner of management. He is a teacher of management. He has seen successes in his own life and in those of others; he has seen failures in his own life and in those of others. (By the way, failures usually teach better lessons than successes.)

Olan is a father and a husband, probably the ultimate test of good management. Olan has been a pastor, often an impossible management situation. Olan has had experience as an executive on numerous levels in diverse circumstances, including being a chief executive officer.

Olan's experience is not limited to the North American continent. He has ministered in seventy-two countries around the world. Many, many times he has been consulted for help in resolving management problems in the farflung corners of the globe.

As the founding executive of the Evangelical Council for Financial Accountability (ECFA), in two years Olan established a new organization and accomplished a task that had never been done in either the secular or Christian community. He established procedures for both internal management and for dealing with hundreds of Christian ministries, and established them well. I know, because I succeeded Olan and have ever been grateful for the excellent base that was left for me to build on.

This book by Olan Hendrix is based on a lifetime of study, practice, and teaching. In the never-ending task of improving management skills, you and I need to add this book to our collection of management books. We need to read it, study it, and refer to it continually. This book is worth the investment of our time, a far more important commodity than our money.

Arthur C. Borden, President
Evangelical Council
    for Financial Accountability

Preface

When I began my ministry some three decades ago, management was the furthest thing from my mind. All I ever wanted to do was preach and teach. And I wanted to do it in China. That was in the mid-forties before China closed its doors to foreigners. My career took strange but exciting and rewarding turns. A total of ten years in the pastorate, ten years on the home staff of a foreign mission society, and almost six years as director of a large home mission preceded serving in Christian publishing, and currently, my work as consultant to Christian organizations worldwide.

Early in my career I found that the ministry involved more than preaching. This book has to do with one, just one, of the often neglected ingredients for a fruitful ministry.

It is easy to see that many of our problems are spiritual. In recent years we have even begun to admit that some are cultural. But how slowly we have come to see that clearly a large segment of our problems are management in nature. This book attempts to offer some help in the latter area only.

This book has a curious history. I delivered some management lectures in Kenya. Then an excited missionary from Zaire typed word-for-word those five days of talks. Later, in 1970, a man from the North of Ireland edited the copy, and a religious publishing company in India printed the first edition. Now this very much revised, updated, and enlarged edition is available.

I am sure that my management thinking has evolved through the years, what with lecturing to well over 35,000 church leaders in eighty countries over a period of nearly thirty years. However, this volume will introduce the subject and will serve as a useful tool to acquaint fellow workers in your church, mission, or other type of Christian organization with management work.

One more thing! Please make no assumptions regarding my personal perfection in the practice of management. I have studied the subject avidly because I needed to. I still need to! All you need to do is ask the people with whom I have worked these years. But I refuse to allow my own management imperfections to deter me from sharing all I can with you. The same principle applies in preaching. Every great preacher preaches beyond his experience. Just as an overdeveloped sense of perfectionism is always one of the greatest enemies to management work, so it could easily silence me on the subject. I refuse!

We face a broken world in unspeakable need. And you and I need all the help we can get. Management skills and tools *can* help.

Olan Hendrix

1 Understand the Problem

The Case for Management in the Christian Organization

It appears to me that management in Christian circles is basically the stewardship of the talents of the persons entrusted to our care.

We are faced with a subject which for some of us is going to be new. Let me suggest the kinds of questions that are going to come to mind. First, "Is the subject of management spiritual, or is it a carnal deviation from trusting the Holy Spirit?" Second, "Is it biblical? Is there a biblical basis for management principles? How can this apply to Christian work?" People often say, "Management is all very good, but how can we apply it when we don't sign the worker's paycheck every week, and don't

13

have the right to fire him or her?" There are definite
answers to these and other questions. Doubts or uncer-
tainties should not prevent us from receiving the instruction which can answer these questions. We can easily
close our minds so that there is no possibility of learning.
Though the subject of Christian management is relatively
new and something of an innovation, clear instruction
and help is available.

Management Defined

First, what do we mean by management? The word
management may sound too authoritative, or too
worldly. Then choose your own word. It does not matter
which word we use as long as we understand what is
meant by—the boss, the director, the superintendent, the
supervisor, the leader, or the manager. The person in
charge of a group of human beings for the accomplishment of a mutually agreed purpose is the manager. In this
book I will use the words *management* and *leadership*
quite interchangeably, although management is a much
more encompassing word of which leadership is just a
part.

The Stewardship of Talents

Let me suggest several definitions. Management in
Christian circles is basically the stewardship of the talents of the persons entrusted to our care. Regardless of
where we are, we work with people. If we are in a position
of leadership, we may not have much to say about who
these people are and we certainly have very little to say
about what their capacities or gifts are. However, we bear
a solemn responsibility to exercise the stewardship of the
talents of those people God has entrusted to our care.
Basically, it is not for us to choose—and we often would
choose people with different capacities if we had the
option—but we do have the responsibility of exercising
careful stewardship of the talents of these people.

In missions and church activities I have observed serious abuse at this point. We often disregard a person's God-given capacity and gifts, sometimes to the satisfaction of our own prejudices, and attempt to force these people into molds or activities for which God the Holy Spirit has not equipped them. Our job as leaders is to exercise Spirit-directed stewardship over these talents. It is for Christian managers to increase to the utmost the performance of those persons whom God has brought into their ranks, taking into account individual gifts and capacities.

Getting Things Done
Through Other People

Lawrence A. Appley says, "Management is getting things done through other people." How is this important for us in Christian work? I am tremendously impressed with this. If ever anything is to be done in this broken world of ours, it is going to be done as we, who are called and sent of God, develop the awareness of the necessity for getting things done through other people. We *must* involve other people. I discovered soon after God saved me that I was never going to be able to accomplish the burden of my own life all by myself. I was going to have to become involved with other people. I couldn't let myself and those entrusted to me do whatever struck my fancy, but *prescribed things* had to be done. It is so much easier, in fact, it is the coward's way out, to conclude that we are going to do what we can do by ourselves and we are not going to worry about what anybody else does.

I had a friend, a pastor of a little church in Maine. He had been there for years preaching to a handful of people. I asked him one day, "What in the world are you doing?" He was doing every menial task in the church, many of which could have been turned over to high school students or other church members. His answer appeared pious and commendable. Actually, it was disheartening.

He said, "I do everything myself. I run off my own bulletins. I wash the windows in the church. I put out the hymn books. I do everything myself. This way I know it is done properly." We must develop the mentality, the attitude, that makes us want to involve other people so that much more can be accomplished and sooner. Jesus Christ did this. Our ministry is not only directed to people but it also involves accomplishing our purpose through people. It is not only *my* ministry to this broken world, but it is my reproducing myself in people with whom I am closely associated so that they minister to this broken world, too. So, by way of definition I would insist that *management for the Christian worker is getting things done through other people.*

Management Is Work and Skill

Basically, management is a set of skills that an ordinary person can acquire and develop. But management may also be thought of as a kind of work which one learns to perform. The important word as we study management is *work*—a kind of work which we perform. The emphasis in the next few pages is going to be on this idea.

You see someone effectively managing or leading a group of people and you are apt to think, "That looks easy. Let me get at it. I can do that." So we jump in and try. Recently friends were visiting us in Philadelphia. I took their teenage boys waterskiing along with my own boys. One boy, about fifteen years old, said, "I'd like to ski too." I asked, "Do you know how, Bobby?" "Oh, yes, yes." So I agreed. He got out and I noticed that when I pulled the rope up taut, his skis were very uncertain, but I thought, "Well, he's a little shaky." Finally he got them straightened out and when I raced the engine, skis and legs and arms went all over the place! I pulled back around, harnessed him up and tried again—and again legs and arms and skis went in all directions. After about the fourth time I pulled back around by him and said, "Bobby, do you know how to ski?" "Yes, I know how to ski." I thought better of the question and said, "Bobby, have you ever skied?" And he replied, "No, but it looks easy." It is that way with leadership. You stand a few feet back and watch a person effectively leading a group and you think, "Oh, that's easy." Just smile, say a few words, write letters, and lead meetings. Give orders and receive reports and it is great—until you try it, and then it is not so easy! It requires skills that very few of us possess naturally.

Now, occasionally a man comes along who can "manage by the seat of his pants!" Let me explain that. Back in World War I, I am told, the pilots in the era preceding the fantastic navigational aids that we enjoy today would determine whether they were flying right side up in the clouds or wrong side up by where the pressure was. If the pressure was on the seat of their pants, they were right side up! If the pressure was on their seat belts, they were wrong side up! Some of us in Christian work manage by the seat of our pants, that is, if it feels right, if it feels comfortable, then it's okay. Or, if intuitively or instinctively we think that is the thing to do or that is not the thing to do, we act accordingly. The problem here is that few people are equipped by conditioning, training, judgment, or personality to manage this way. This is why we need to learn specific leadership skills. We must identify and then acquire these skills. We are looking at Christian management as work to be performed, as skills to be acquired.

On one occasion my six-year-old boy was trying to learn to ride a bicycle. Oh, what mistakes! I got him going, and he'd bang into the side of the house or into a tree or something else! One day he said, "Daddy, it looks so easy but it's hard." "It does look easy, John, but there are things you have to do. You have to keep going. You have to keep the wheels going in the right direction. You need to steer and feel the balance. When you feel the bike going one way you have to pull back the other way." He said,

"Yes, but it looks so easy." There are a lot of things that look easy but they require learning certain skills. There are times when we develop these skills to where they become second nature. They become instinctive. We are not conscious that we are practicing these skills—like riding a bicycle. After a while, though, it becomes second nature. We just do it—but first we learn the skill and then we abide by the rules.

Tools for Spiritual Persons

Management is a skill, but it is also a set of tools for spiritual persons. Management tools can be used by people who are not spiritual for ulterior and worldly purposes. But, by the same token, spiritual people can take these tools and use them for the glory of God and for the furtherance of the work of Jesus Christ. The point is not whether or not these tools are spiritual—*the whole point is whether or not WE are spiritual.* Let us not argue with the skills or the tools but with the condition of our own hearts. The issue is, "Am I a spiritual person?" If so, these tools can be worthwhile and powerful implements in my hands.

Now if you want to be carnal in your service for Jesus Christ, you do not have to use management skills to be so. In a slovenly way, in a haphazard way, you can be carnal. The using of these skills does not mean that you are carnal, nor does the absence of them mean that you are spiritual. Be careful about that assumption.

Management As a Supplement

Here is a quotation that I want to sink so deeply into your consciousness that you will never, never forget it! An Ohio pastor made this observation—*"There are some things God will bless as a supplement that He will curse as a substitute."* I am not talking about management skills as a substitution for anything.

Often people will wonder:

"Isn't this a substitute for the fullness of the Holy Spirit?" No!

"Isn't this a bypassing of the responsibilities for the exposition of the Word?" No!

"Isn't this a shortcut to try to circumvent the necessity for believers being drawn together in spiritual unity?" No!

Management is not a substitute for anything. It is a *supplement*. It is a set of tools for spiritual persons.

It is so important that we understand one another, that we get started off right and on the right foundation. The issue is not the spirituality of management. The issue is the spirituality of the person. We spend our lives arguing about the spirituality of things. Things are not spiritual; people are.

Management in the Bible

Is the subject of management scriptural? Is it biblical? Can we honestly study this subject giving the Word of God the preeminence in guiding our thinking? I think we can. I believe that every basic, honorable principle in management has its root and foundation in the Word of God.

Joseph

Take, for example, the life of Joseph. Is there in all of history a more magnificent example of leadership and good management than Joseph? Preparing for that monumental harvest, then the horrible years of famine, delegating, planning the whole operation, distributing the materials, the foodstuffs, satisfying the complaints, and handling the grievances—all the challenges are there. The people he had to work with were no better than the people you and I work with. As a matter of fact, he might have had worse people than some of us have. His leadership is a magnificent example of organization. And did God just drop it down into his brain so that he did it instinctively without ever thinking? I do not think so. God seldom works that way with us. Generally, he will guide us to the subjects we need to study and learn.

Nehemiah

Or take Nehemiah and his exploits. If you read the Book of Nehemiah carefully, and seek to find the management principles in it, you will discover that it contains every major management principle we know about today.

If I were to give a biblical exposition on the subject of management I would unhesitatingly turn to the Book of Nehemiah. It is all there in lucid and succinct form.

Jesus

Is there organization in Scripture? I think so. Dr. Robert Coleman in his book, *The Master Plan of Evangelism,* studies the life of the Lord Jesus in his relationship with the apostles, and shows his selection of them, then his association with them: impartation, demonstration, delegation, supervision, and reproduction. There were intense organizational activities in the life of the Lord Jesus and in his relations with his disciples. Of course, the classic source of information regarding the Lord and his twelve is the volume by A. B. Bruce, *The Training of the Twelve.*

Moses

I attended a management seminar taught by Louis A. Allen, a noted management researcher. When he came to the subject of delegation he said, "I've got one example of delegation for you—Moses." This is a classic example of delegation in the Word of God. Delegation did not solve all the problems for Moses, but it solved some of the major ones. It created some others, but when we solve one problem, we create other problems. In fact, the last question to always ask yourself when you implement a decision to solve a problem is, "What is going to go wrong when I implement this decision?"

Confident Christian Leadership

I want to point out something about management in the church of the Lord Jesus Christ. It would mean a lot to the security of our people if they looked to us and found us confident. "This is the work God has given me to do." It is biblical, is it not? God gives these various capacities to us and then he gives us to the Church for specific purposes (Eph. 4:11–12). Romans 12:8 says, "Or he that exhorteth, let him wait on exhortation; he that giveth, let him do it with simplicity; he that ruleth, with diligence." (KJV) The Cambridge Bible says *ruleth* means to "preside whether in church or in any point of the work." It goes on to say that *with diligence* means "in haste, with earnestness, with laborious and minute attention to duty."

It is always interesting to me that we are so apologetic in our attitude toward our positions of responsibility. Why is this? I think there are some psychological reasons for it. We need to put our shoulders back and hold our heads high and say, "I am the pastor, I am the leader, I am whatever I am by the appointment of a sovereign God." We often underestimate ourselves and allow others to value us below God's estimation of us. I am not suggesting that we grasp after position. We are not to count the position as something to be grasped. No, we are to have the mind of Christ. But we are not talking about status. We are talking about work, about a divine assignment of work and a performance of skills. What happens if we belittle our ability and position? One of the reasons we are in trouble in evangelicalism is because we have underestimated our leadership ability.

Why Has Management Been Neglected?

The next thing to consider is "Why is management neglected?" The first reason is *ignorance*. We simply do not know how to manage. It never occurred to most of us to study leadership as a set of skills that might be acquired like one would study apologetics or hermeneutics. My orientation was preaching. That is all I ever wanted to do. But, I got out of bed one morning and found myself a manager! I was not alone; other people in our mission were in the same boat. What does one do? You "fly by the seat of your pants!" You do what you feel is right, or what you think is right, or what you hope is right. Of course, you pray and ask for guidance, but basically you are ignorant of what to do.

One day one of my board members came along and said, "Olan, you are in trouble." I knew that. My only consolation was that I was not alone. Our mission had outgrown a very satisfactory form of management. Normally an organization comes into being with a certain form of government. However, it will outgrow the demand for that style of leadership and demand a new style of leadership as it goes through various structures and stages. This is why most organizations emerge, flourish, and then founder! They cannot make the transition into a new era. We were in real trouble—demoralization had set in. Our best men were threatening to leave. Our form of government seemed to be working against us.

So this board member came along and said, "If I pay your way to a management seminar, will you go?" Well, at that point I would have jumped off a bridge if I thought it would have helped. We were in trouble. So I attended a seminar, and as I listened to the leader talk about the application of management principles to cooperative human efforts I said, "That will work! That is our problem! There is where we have missed it!" The ignorance began to be dispelled. It was not easy. I had a lot of ingrained prejudices and I had to overcome them, and I am still having to overcome them.

The Strong Natural Leader

Another reason why we neglect the subject of management is that our traditional concept of leadership in the church is the strong natural leader. Now when God saved me and called me to preach, all I wanted to do was preach. I wanted to learn how to preach, and especially how to be a missionary. Later, when I knew I could not go to China, I wanted to learn how to be a pastor. I thought to myself, "I am going to learn how to preach and how to get things done." So I went away to college. And, lo and behold, at this college there was a strong natural leader in charge. The college was also in close proximity to a large church. I decided I was going to watch how the leader became so great.

He would get up in church and let his congregation have it straight from the shoulder! I decided I could do the same thing. So when I got the opportunity to preach out in a small country church, I would get up and let them have it straight from the shoulder, and they would toss me out by my ear! I would then pull myself together and go back the next Sunday to observe him and say, "I'll watch some more. I missed something." Again, he would let them have it straight from the shoulder. I have seen that man get up and call on four or five deacons to pray when he knew they were not there, just to embarrass them in front of two thousand people. Well, what I did not know was that this man was a strong natural leader, and he can't be copied.

A student came along one time when I was in college, looked at my library such as it was, and said, "Look, all you have is Greek, Hebrew, apologetics, and philosophy. Where are your biographies?" I replied, "Why do I need them? I am going to preach." He said, "You need to read biographies." So I went out and bought some biographies and autobiographies. You know, most biographies are written about strong natural leaders. They did not help me. Reading those biographies hindered me. I found myself spending some nights in prayer, asking God to make me one of them. I did not know the term *strong natural leader* then but I had Wesley, Taylor, Studd, Whitefield,

Edwards, Spurgeon, and others in mind. I wanted to be
like them.

That is bondage. You have to accept yourself as you are.
It was like getting out of jail when I awakened one day to
discover that God wants me just as I am. I am not talking
in a moral sense but in the sense of personality and
capacity. God has made me as I am. God has equipped me
as I am equipped. He has divided these gifts to every man
according to his wisdom. Well, this was wonderful! But
how slow I was to recognize this.

Strong natural leaders are often successful—highly successful—but usually only over a short period of time.
Unless they die or are displaced, they often become their
organization's worst enemy. I was glad to discover that I
was not a strong natural leader.

There is an alternative, and the alternative is the pro-
fessional leader, the scientific leader or the developed
leader. I mean, people who do not have the dominating
personality to draw others to themselves automatically,
to cause others to do what they want them to do. Instead,
they are the persons who are ordinary human beings like
you or me who develop leadership skills and engage in
this management work.

Now, I am not concerned with strong natural leaders.
They seldom attend a leadership conference or read a
management book. They feel they do not need to. Ordinary persons like you and me who are in positions of
leadership can develop extensive leadership skills. We
will deal with that point in the coming chapter: how to
develop these skills. We will also discover how to implement these skills in our own situations.

2 Identify Responsibilities

The Functions and Activities of Management

In management, and especially in Christian management, you never come to the place where you can say, "I am finished." You are not building a table or a chair; you are working with lives, with human beings, with minds, with emotions, with hearts, with frail bodies subject to all the pressures of an ever-changing world.

Every activity involved in any managerial situation can be plugged in under one of the following four main headings or one of the nineteen subpoints.[1] This is true in

1. Allen, Louis A. *The Management Profession.* (New York: McGraw-Hill) p. 68.

a highly complex managerial situation, such as General Motors, or in a simple situation. Even two people working together to accomplish a mutually agreed objective must accomplish the same activities.

1. **Function:** Management Planning
   Activities: Estimating the future, Establishing objectives, Developing policies, Programming, Establishing procedures, Scheduling, Budgeting
2. **Function:** Management Organizing
   Activities: Developing organization structure, Delegating, Establishing interpersonal human relationships
3. **Function:** Management Leading
   Activities: Decision making, Communicating, Motivating, Selecting people, Developing people
4. **Function:** Management Controlling
   Activities: Establishing performance standards, Performance measuring, Performance evaluating, Performance correcting

The outline has four parts (Louis Allen calls them functions): planning, organizing, leading, and controlling. My purpose is to discuss this list, defining the terms very briefly, with the hope that we can look into these subjects individually and see how they relate to Christian work.

This grouping is not in any particular order. You do not plan before you organize or before you lead or before you develop. You can even set up a management file just like this: planning, leading, organizing, and controlling. It makes a good acrostic—PLOC. I have a file for each of these main points and each of the subpoints. Everytime I find something on the subject of management that I want to retain, I file it in one of these places. Everything written on the subject of management can fit easily into one of these slots.

What do we mean by these terms? Here are some very brief definitions.

1. Management Planning

Planning is the work we do to predetermine a course of action. Or, planning is throwing a net over tomorrow to cause the thing we want to come to pass. The alternative to planning is chance and just letting things happen as they will.

Estimating the future is the work we do to anticipate what tomorrow is going to be like. Many of us say we do not know this because things change so rapidly. This is precisely the reason why we need to engage in the work of estimating. The rapidity with which changes are taking place today summons us to appraise as accurately as possible what tomorrow is going to be like.

The principal resource for doing this difficult work is the study of trends that affect our organizations. Trends are not infallible but they are the best indicator we have.

Establishing objectives is the work we do to determine goals or targets. Any Christian organization that has been in existence for more than twenty years usually has no goals, just activities.

The hardest work we have to do in being the heart of an organization is determining cooperatively meaningful objectives. I seldom meet a pastor who can answer in a few words, "Pastor, what is the objective of your church? Why is your church in existence?" You would be surprised how much confusion there is regarding goals and objectives in Christian work. This, more than anything else, contributes to our ineffectiveness. We can be filled with the Holy Spirit and not have definitive goals in our work.

Developing policies is the work of formulating standing answers to recurring questions. Normally in Christian work we confuse policies and objectives. A potential missionary candidate will often ask, "What are your mission policies?" What he or she usually means is, "What are your mission objectives?"

Programming is the establishing of the priority and sequence of activities for the accomplishment of our goals or objectives. Objectives should always sit in judgment on activities.

Procedures is the standardizing of the methods of work. We in Christian work are easily lax in this area. A young man or woman is thrown into a work and told to do it, but is not allowed to benefit from what has been previously learned by other people who have gone into similar types of work. Everybody should benefit from what others have learned about a particular type of work. I have actually seen this sort of thing happen: A young missionary out of language study is assigned a town and told, "Start a church here." Start a church? What do I do now? Here is a town completely secularized and materialistic and pre-occupied, feeling no need of God or the Gospel, and this young person is supposed to start a church. No one says, "Here is all we have learned from what we have been doing so far. We still do not know everything, but here is what little we do know. We want you to benefit from it so that you can get the job done most economically in time and effort."

Scheduling is the work of putting a time factor on our program and inserting the calendar into the program with dates, hours, and minutes. Attempt to understand the mind of the Lord when he expects a certain thing done and then try to cooperate with the Holy Spirit.

Budgeting concerns more than just money! A new convert was asked by the treasurer of our mission, "What are your impressions of missionaries?" He had several. This man, an advertising executive, said, "The missionaries that I have met put proper evaluation on money, but no evaluation on time." I agree. We are talking about budgeting personnel, time, and equipment, as well as money. Budgeting is the application of all of our resources.

2. Management Organizing

Organizing is the work of grouping people and work so the work can best be performed by human beings. Whenever we think of organizing, we think of something like charts, blocks, lines: these blocks representing people and titles: director, superintendent, chairman, supervisor, and so on. Organizing is tying together activities under one person for the accomplishment of a specific goal. Organizing is necessary to prevent fragmentation and the dissipation of activities and energies. Unless we organize, we have people doing what is noble and right and good and commendable, but not bringing into strict discipline all of the activities of their lives and resources to accomplish a purpose. Organizing does not have to be complicated. It does not make any difference how we do it, whether or not we have a chart. It means each person knows what work he or she is definitively responsible for. There are three aspects to organizing.

Developing organizational structure occurs when we group and relate work and people to one another. This involves relating people one to another in their performance and in their authority, not just in responsibility.

Delegation causes more misunderstanding perhaps than any other single aspect of management. Delegating is the assigning of things:

1. Responsibility, or if you prefer, work.
2. Authority, that is, showing people how much authority they have, what kind of decisions they can make, and how far they can go. They must not only know what they are to do, but how much money they can spend, how many decisions they can make, how many people they can direct or control, and how much time they can devote to it.
3. Accountability, establishing lines of reporting. The person who delegates not only says, "Will you do this piece of work?" and "Here is the authority you

need in order to perform that job." He or she also
says, "I will check back with you Friday afternoon at
two o'clock to see how you are making out."

We frequently fail to establish lines of accountability
and delegation because we are afraid of people. Management involves us "eyeball to eyeball" with people in
direct personal encounter. It takes time. We like to think
we are too busy preaching and teaching to perform management work.

If we will harmoniously blend these three ingredients
in delegation, we can tremendously improve the performance of our organization. But remember, we must have
all three components for success: responsibility, authority, and accountability.

*Establishing and maintaining interpersonal relation-
ships* is management organizing. Those little boxes that
we draw and those words that we write on paper and the
nice neat little job descriptions that we make—all that is
wonderful, except when we forget one thing—they represent people! People become ill, people become offended,
people get tired, people become depressed. If you do not
like both people and people's problems, *get out of management.* It is better that you leave management to somebody else if your attitude, when a problem emerges or
when a person fails, is, "Will these people never learn?"
Your attitude should be like that of the Lord Jesus to his
disciples.

A. B. Bruce brings this Jesus attitude out very clearly in
his book, *The Training of the Twelve.* Christ taught the
disciples that same thing over and over again. Finally they
began to grasp a little bit of what he was trying to say.
Teaching must be done day after day. In management, and
especially in Christian management, you never come to
the place where you can say, "I am finished." You are not
building a table or a chair; you are working with lives,
with human beings, with minds, with emotions, with

hearts, with frail bodies subject to all the pressures of an ever-changing world.

3. Management Leading

Of all four functions, management leading is the most work and the least mechanical. When it comes to leading, we are much more involved with interpersonal relationships. Management leading is the work we do to inspire and to impel people to take specific action. It involves five areas:

Decision making, or problem identification and solving, is the work we do to arrive at judgments and conclusions. Decision making is not simply intuition. There is a specific process in which we engage to arrive at logical judgments and conclusions. Decision making is not mystical. In fact, a mystic can make some very bad judgments. Because we have feelings at a gut level does not insure that we are going to arrive at proper judgments and conclusions.

Communicating is the work we engage in to arrive at an understanding between ourselves and other people concerning mutual needs and goals. Beware of confusing understanding with agreement. We suffer infinitely more management ill from misunderstanding than from disagreement.

Motivating is one of the biggest subjects on the list. This is the work we do to cause people to want to do what needs to be done. Remember, significant motivating work is done one-on-one much more than in groups.

Selecting people is the work we engage in to appraise people's God-given capacities and the opportunities available to fit them. We try to find work for which individuals are best suited. How many misplaced Christian workers there are!

Developing people has to do with the work we do to
upgrade the capacities for work and service which
have been given by the Holy Spirit. Here is a person
who has been equipped or gifted to do something
special. To develop him or her, we help enlarge those
capacities and then build on them. This is developing
people.

4. Management Controlling

Controlling is the work done to insure that results
conform to plan. Controlling presupposes both objectives
and a specific structure. Management controlling includes four activities:

Establishing performance standards means that we
agree with the person or the persons working with us
as to what quality work is going to be accomplished,
before it is begun. There is a mutual agreement. Here
is the job and here is the standard to which it is going
to be performed. Many problems arise at this point.
We give people a job or ask them to do something.
They assume, "This is not very important. We can do
it sloppily or half-heartedly. It does not really matter." We, however, attach a great deal of significance
to it. We must communicate adequately so that we
and our workers agree about the standard for the job;
otherwise there is going to be incompatibility and
serious friction. We must establish performance
standards. If new assistants are assigned to you, let
them know what you expect of them. Many breaches
of relationships occur because of failure to communicate expectations.

Performance measuring means that whether people are
counting money, passing out literature on the street,
planting a church in a pioneer area, or whatever they
are doing, somebody is measuring their work. Now,
the point here is not to measure how many souls they

have led to Christ; it is their performance in their work that is to be measured, and it may or may not be reflected in souls saved. We have built-in resistance when we attempt to do this.

Performance evaluating is the appraisal of the importance of an individual's work in relation to all the other work which is being performed in the organization, and with respect to accomplishing the total goal. When we get into this kind of thing seriously, we will find a lot of people doing jobs that do not need to be done.

Performance correcting involves not only correcting mistakes that have been made but also involves coaching, providing the person with the "how." It is saying, "Here is how you do it," and then coming back to correct mistakes and to continually provide methods for accomplishing the assigned task. We do not have to know how to do it ourselves, but we have to know where to send people for the help they need to learn how to do it. Performance correcting includes coaching. In other words, we do not just set standards, and measure and evaluate. We also coach: "Read that book." "Take that course." "Talk to that person." "Read this article."

According to L. A. Allen, the above activities constitute the totality of the management process in any and all situations. Your first love is likely to be preaching or teaching, but you have an inescapable responsibility to serve your people by doing management work for them. And if you do not incorporate this work in your life, the entire organization will suffer.

3 Get Organized

The Basic Organizational Orientations

Generally, religious organizations start out with a goal orientation, deteriorate to a task orientation, and finally degenerate to the bottom—to control orientation.

I now wish to draw your attention to something that is foundational to management. There are three basic types of organizational orientation or organizational mentalities.

The Task Mentality

First, there is *task* orientation which says, "Do this, do that, do something else." Task orientation is primarily concerned with the performance and activity of the moment, and not with the distant goal. The task mentality is revealed in the following illustration with which I am sure you are all acquainted. A man walked up to several workmen.

He asked one workman, "What are you doing?"

"I'm laying bricks."

He addressed another, "What are you doing?"

"I am installing glass."

Finally, he spoke to a man who was wheeling a wheelbarrow, "What are you doing?"

"I'm building a cathedral."

All of these men except the last had a task orientation. In industry the task orientation expresses itself this way: "Put that nut on that bolt. Never mind what you are building. Just put that nut on that bolt." The average church or mission has a task orientation. "Here is what we do. Here is the activity in which we are engaged."

The Control Mentality

Control orientation is concerned primarily with government, authority, and decisions. The most important thing about our association is to make sure that control is maintained, that a proper form of government is perpetuated, and that we do things to a certain standard. Control says it does not make any difference whether we accomplish anything or not, but let us make sure that *we do it right*.

The Goal Mentality

Goal orientation says government, authority, procedure, precedent, and history must serve a specific purpose. Everything that is done (task) must strategically contribute to the stated goal. Goal orientation is obsessed with clearly defined objectives. Everything else is subservient to the objective. This is the hardest orientation to maintain. Generally, religious organizations start out with a goal orientation, deteriorate to a task orientation, and finally degenerate to the bottom—to control orientation.

I have been talking about evangelical ecumenicity for a long time and have been cited about ecumenicity within a predetermined theological framework. One day I was talking with a lady about her mission. She was the head of a small but prominent mission. But, they had not had a new missionary in eight years and they were deteriorating. They were not growing in any way and yet they were perpetuating their old structures. They had degenerated to the bottom, to the control pattern. I said to her, "Dear lady, why don't you merge your mission with somebody who can bring vitality and help to the areas where you need it so the people involved in your work can accomplish the goals to which they originally committed themselves?" "Oh, merge! We could not merge. That would be an invasion of the sanctity of the origin of our mission." What she was really saying was, "We have no goal other than the perpetuation of our form." Perpetuate she will, and sadly enough, so will her constituency!

It is very easy to substitute sentiment for organizational purpose. Identifying goals can lead to a fierce battle. Our job, in part, is to lead our followers back to a goal orientation.

Is this biblical? Yes, indeed: "Forgetting those things which are behind and reaching forth unto those things which are before, I press toward the mark for the prize of the high calling of God in Christ Jesus" (Phil. 3:13,14). "What mean ye to weep and break my heart? For I am ready not to be bound only, but also to die at Jerusalem for the name of the Lord Jesus" (Acts 21:13). "I'm ready to preach" (Rom. 1:15). "He steadfastly set his face to go to Jerusalem" (Luke 9:51). It is very biblical. I may only lay bricks with one hand and wield a sword with the other, but I am going to build the wall.

Our spiritual degeneration has taken us down this bitter road to task and control orientation to the exclusion of our goal orientation. Some of us in our organizations will have a bitter struggle to ever regain a goal orientation. Sometimes it cannot be regained in an organization. Maybe you have heard of the inevitable cycle in religious organizations. It starts with a *man* (or woman) with a vision and a burden. Thus it becomes a *movement*, and this generally degenerates into a *machine*. Then, finally, it becomes a *monument*. These are the four "M's" of organizational deterioration and it results in "control organization." This mentality says in effect, "Never mind whether we are doing anything; let us just make sure that we are doing it properly!"

The best way we have discovered to get things done through a group of people committed to a common objective is to have someone within the group do the work of planning, leading, organizing, and controlling.

Two Principles

The *principle of ministry priority* teaches us that when we are called on to perform both management and ministry work during the same period, we tend to give first priority to ministry work. Let me illustrate. Here you have a group of church planters, evangelists, in a given situation, country, or province. These people, however few or many, are banded together to do church-planting. The purpose of this organization is to evangelize with the view to establishing local groups of believers in this province or city. One man is put in the position of chairman, manager, superintendent, director, or whatever you want to call him. This man will plan, lead, organize, and control in behalf of the group. Ministry work is preaching, evangelizing, conducting meetings, visiting, handing out literature, making disciples, and so on. Now, when this man who is skilled in ministry is put in a managerial position, and is required to both minister and manage at the same time, he will tend to give preference to ministry rather than to managing.

It is important to understand the difference between ministry and managing. This principle could apply to a machine shop where there are three men operating pieces of machinery. One of them is made the manager, but he is also required to operate a machine at the same time. He will tend to let the work of management slip in deference to the operating work every time.

When ministers are put in positions of management, the constant temptation is to minister rather than to manage. We will always sermonize. We will always go out and meet people and talk with people. We will do anything before we manage. And this is disastrous in its final results because it throws the group into chaos and confusion. You meet these symptoms when a person who should be managing is exclusively ministering. People commonly say, "Well, I don't know what we are here for. I don't know what he is doing." People will constantly suspect other persons, activities and motives when there is lack of management. Lack of management leads to frustration and results in people casting their minds back to the "good old days when there was just Joe and Bill and me out here and we knew what we were doing. But it is all changed now." The cause is a lack of management.

The principle of *organizational levels* teaches us that the lower the organizational level, the more ministry work a manager is able to perform. Now, conversely, the higher the organizational level, the more a man is required to manage. I do not think this needs any enlargement. Where you are on the management level determines how much of your time should be spent in

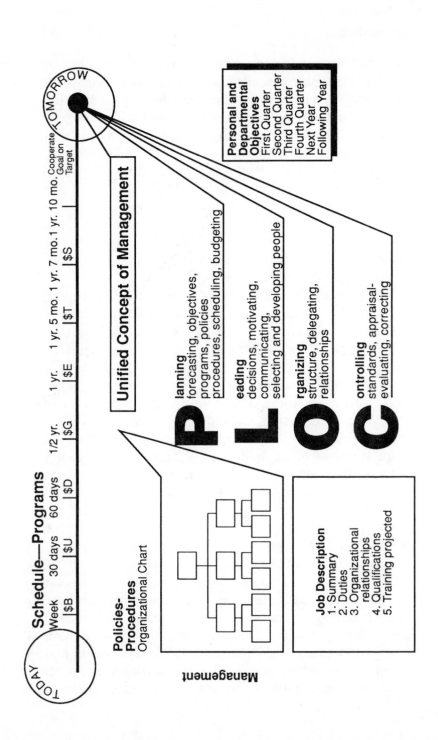

planning, leading, organizing, and controlling. It is very interesting to note that the Christian world at large is not quite ready to accept management as work. We accept it as a reward for faithfulness or stature or achievement, but do not see it as work.

Because we are not geared in our mentality to accept management as a type of work for Christian organization, we do not require people to have training in this sphere. We do not set people aside and say, "Your job is to plan, lead, organize, and control."

What if you hired a man to paint your house and he came with ladders, paint, and paint brushes and sat down and said, "Well, it needs painting all right, but I think I will drink some coffee." And he drank coffee for four hours. Then he said, "That house sure needs painting and I know I ought to paint it. Somebody has to paint it, but I think I will work in the garden. I like flowers."

Well, this could be stretched on and on. The point is, he is not doing what he is supposed to do. We will try to discover as we go along why we avoid management work.

4 Devise the Plans

Planning—Its Characteristics and Principles

Informed planning is based on the fact that phenomena do not occur singly. Everything comes preceded by many other things, accompanied by many things, and followed by many things. The cause-and-effect relationship of things is the most important natural law we have. Planning, therefore, is doing specified work today to cause desired results tomorrow.

Louis A. Allen in *The Management Profession* defines planning as, "the work a manager performs to predetermine a course of action." According to him, the all-encompassing view of planning includes the following:

1. *Forecasting*: Estimate the future.
2. *Establishing objectives*: Determine the end results to be accomplished with the people involved.
3. Programming: Establish the sequence and priority of action-steps to be followed in reaching objectives.
4. *Scheduling*: Establish a time sequence for program steps.
5. *Budgeting*: Allocate resources necessary to accomplish objectives.
6. *Procedure*: Develop and apply standardized methods of performing specific work.
7. *Policies*: Develop and interpret standing decisions that apply to recurrent questions and problems of significance to the enterprise as a whole.

What all this says is that planning is one of the most important words in the management functions. Always vital in successful management, planning has assumed unparalleled importance in these days of jet-swift change. Abraham Lincoln said in 1858, "If we could first know where we are, and whither we are tending, we could better judge what to do and how to do it." Informed planning is based on the fact that phenomena do not occur singly. Everything comes preceded by many other things. The cause-and-effect relationship of things is the most important natural law we have. Planning, therefore, is doing specified work today to cause desired results tomorrow.

Planning Is Difficult

Why do we have such difficulty with planning? A vice-president of the Westinghouse Company said, "Today the world is changing so rapidly that we cannot train to meet a given situation. We must educate people to cope with whatever changes may occur." Here is where we have failed in Christian work. We have trained pastors to meet issues that we faced fifteen years ago. Those battles have been fought. Now, we must educate people to cope with whatever changes may occur in the future, and there are only three things about the future, that we are certain of:

1. The future will not be like the past.
2. The future will not be like we think it is going to be.
3. The rate of change will be faster than ever before.

Look again so that you can see all the components of planning. These things fit together like a piece of fine machinery. You can take them out and examine them one at a time, but for a plan to work, all of the seven components listed above have to fit together like a piece of machinery.

Decisions Made in Advance

With these seven parts of planning in mind, consider the characteristics of planning. The first characteristic is that planning consists of decisions made in advance of action. Are you aware how difficult decision making is for the average human being? I saw a cartoon some time ago. A girl was speeding along the road in her car and she came to a fork in the road. There was a sign in the island in the middle of the diverging roads that said, "Take either road." She ran into the post in the middle. As she climbed out of the car and spoke to the policeman the caption read, "I couldn't make up my mind which one to take."

Indecisiveness is one of the greatest enemies of management. A person comes into my office and says, "I would like to talk to you about our work, our organization. We cannot get decisions. Nobody wants to decide. Everybody seeks to avoid responsibility." Often the person will say, "We have to write to New York, Chicago, or London, or to somewhere else to get a decision, and this demoralizes people terribly."

Planning is difficult because planning says, "Today we are deciding many issues related to the future." Planning involves decisions made in advance of action. Nothing so reveals courage and direction on the part of a Christian worker like serious planning. We are certain of what God wants us to accomplish. We are committed under the direction of the Holy Spirit to a certain thing. These are the decisions necessary to move in this direction. If you fire a bullet toward a bull's-eye, it is very difficult to catch up with it and change its course. Actually, we would often prefer to be without purpose rather than to select a purpose that commits us in a definite direction. Today's purposes, aims, and decisions commit us tomorrow, and next month, and next year.

The Behavior of People

The second characteristic of planning is that it deals with future *behavior of people*. Do not assume that the people you deal with are any different than the people that anyone else deals with in the world, in industry, in business, or in another country.

A man asked me after I had been in Africa about a day and a half, "What are your impressions of Africa?" "Well," I said, "I have none yet except that it is like every other place I have ever been in. It is full of people!"

As trite as it sounds, people are an amazingly common denominator. In these past few years, as I have traveled and observed missions in many situations and have met missionaries who come from all over the world, I have been amazed. As we talked we could narrow the problems down to a small list. They are basically the same in every country, and the greatest problem is: "We deal with people." Do not say, "Well, it is different in industry." No, it is precisely the same. I have gone to industrial management seminars and listened to people in industrial settings grapple with the same problems that we grapple with in our work. Industrialists ask precisely the same questions we ask. When we plan, we are deciding now that other people will carry out specified actions at future periods. This means we have to coordinate, motivate, channel, guide, and communicate without fail.

One of the most important things we can learn about the future behavior of people is found in a catchy phrase: *take people action.* The principle is, if you expect someone to cooperate with you later in doing something, involve them now in the decision to do it. Two of the most important aspects of planning, dealing with the future behavior of people, are these: conditioning and timing.

We must condition people! Remember, management on the part of the Christian worker is never a partner to subterfuge or insincerity or anything that is the slightest bit dishonest or misrepresentative. Never! Conditioning does not mean deceiving people or hood-winking them or pulling the wool over their eyes. Conditioning means giving people information so that they know the facts. It means involving them in everything you know about the situation.

People hate secretiveness on the part of a leader. Why is a person secretive? Because his or her ego craves to know something that somebody else does not know.

R. E. Thompson, chairman of the board of the Far Eastern Gospel Crusade for many years, founder of Missionary Internship, and a missionary to China says, "Tell your people everything you can tell them and they will seldom demand that you tell them what you should not tell them. There is a place for secrets, but if you will tell your people all you can, you will seldom find them asking you to tell them what you should not tell them."

How you go about telling depends on the subject matter and the situation at hand. Some things can be adequately conveyed in a memorandum or a letter, but letters are poor vehicles for communication. The best way, of course, is face to face; but the larger the group, the bigger the problem. Leaders should take advantage of every op-

portunity with people to condition them, and if they
faithfully do so, people will not resent leaders when they
forget. One of the manager's jobs is to condition people
for the inevitable change that is coming down the road.
God revealed his ways to Moses and his acts to the children of Israel. The person at the top must constantly be
conditioning the people below. Take every opportunity to
do so.

The other aspect of dealing with the behavior of people
is *timing*. There is a time question: When? The immature
leader always feels it must be done now; and if it cannot
be done now, a personal affront is taken. That is imma-
turity. I remember one time as a pastor I had a bright idea.
The only problem was that it occurred to me on Monday
and we were having our annual business meeting on
Wednesday. So, I sprung it on the congregation! Do you
know what happened? They threw it out. Because it was a
bad idea? No, it was a good one. A year later they accepted
the idea with no problem. What was wrong? My timing
was off. When we are planning for the future behavior of
people, we must have both condition and time. Know
well in advance definitely where you are going.

The Role of Change

The third characteristic is that planning involves
change. I am convinced that change is the most evident
characteristic of our time and I am also convinced that the
average Christian worker is oblivious to it. Some of us are
living as if conditions were the same today as twenty-five
years ago. We are as out of touch as we can be. We are not
aware of the changes that have developed around us.
American Management Association President, Lawrence
Appley, described how rapidly changes develop this way:
"We are confronted with the rate of change—it is the rate
of change of change." It is no longer the rate of change, it
is the rate of change of change! Alvin Toffler's best-selling
book, *Future Shock*, discusses this at great length. Change

is taking place very rapidly and it is touching you and the people you are working with. You might occasionally think, *Oh, I am living in a city or village where change will not affect us.* Don't believe it! Technology has advanced more in the last fifty years than in the preceding five thousand years and in the next five years we will double our technological advance. Very few Christian workers are able to adapt to the demands of this kind of change in society.

Consider for a moment the following. More people are alive on the earth today than have died since mankind first appeared. Some experts are predicting that by the year 2,000 we will have instant worldwide television communication. Many of the countries of the world will proudly display automated highways. These are already in the experimental stages. Fish will be herded and raised in off-shore pens in the ocean to feed the population. There will be automatic atomic and hydrogen controls. Drugs will alter basic personality patterns in the individual. Eric Hoffer in his book, *The Ordeal of Change,* says, "Nobody really likes the new. We all fight change. Taking a new step, uttering a new word, is what people fear the most." And for people like you and me, the issue is *change or die.*

In 1960 the Gallup Poll in the United States revealed that 14 percent of the population felt that the church in America was irrelevant and unrelated to real life situations. In 1967 the same poll showed that 54 percent of the population said the church was unrelated to society. We are being pressed in a corner these days to see if we are really going to adapt to meet the needs of a changing world.

I was conducting a week of meetings in a seaside town where people come in large crowds during the summer. They stay in hotels and tourist homes and swim in the ocean all day. I was preaching in a very conservative church. An innovative evangelistic group was having meetings there. They had about 60–70 students working through the summer trying to evangelize the young drop-out crowd. I was invited to observe their efforts, so I said to myself, "I'm going to work with these people." After the service I tried to look contemporary. I took my tie off and pulled my shirt tail out and looked as sloppy as I could. I would slouch down the street and go to what they called their "Hunger Hangar," the place where they had psychedelic posters on the windows and walls. Well, I had the time of my life.

I found a whole segment of the population that rejected the Church. Two of these fellows walked into the church where I was preaching, toward the end of the meeting. They had scruffy beards, were smoking cigarettes and smelled unpleasantly! You could have heard a pin drop. The people were standing around in their nice clothes, staring at them. "What are they doing here?" Well, I knew the fellows, so I went to the back of the church and greeted them. "Hello, how are you?" I shook hands with them and everybody stared dumbfoundedly. "What's going on? Who are they?" Do you know who they are? They are representatives of a great segment of this world, to which we need to adapt so that we can win them to Christ.

Someone once said, "Difficulties result when attachments, proper to faith, are transferred uncritically to methods of work." It is our ideological dogmatism, our theoretically unsupported assertions, that get us into trouble. We think that because something worked in the past, it is going to work in the present. But it might not work in our day at all. It depends on whether our emphasis is task, control, or goal. That is what makes the difference.

Emerson lamented, "Improved means to unimproved ends." Einstein concurred: "Few things so characterize our day as perfection of means and confusion of goals." That is the world. The world often perfects and improves means to uncertain or less than noble ends; the church pursues noble ends, but with antiquated means. Change! Change anything, change everything that can be changed to accomplish our goal. Now does this mean we change our theology? No! I am not suggesting that. I am saying that in our planning we should come up with such a commitment to a goal that we consider everything, old and new, in the light of achieving that goal.

Why Do We Not Plan?

Why do we not make the effort that is required to establish objectives, estimate the future program, establish budgets and procedures? What are the barriers to this planning? Let me suggest that the first reason is simply that we do not know how. Some of us do not plan because we have never seen it done.

Secondly, we do not plan because most of us prefer to do things than to think about them. Planning is thinking. Planning is coordinating. Planning is analyzing. Planning is communicating. Planning is interacting. Planning is revising, appraising, criticizing, and it is easier to act than to think about it.

Thirdly, the barrier to planning is the uncertainty of the future. We do not know what tomorrow is going to be like. So we tend to say, "Oh, what is the use? Every time I make plans they go astray. So I am just not going to plan any more." That is limited perspective and reveals a task-orientation rather than goal-orientation. Goal-orientation will continually say, "Here is the thing we are committed to achieve." We have to keep revising and regrouping and bringing pressures to bear so that all of the activities aim toward the goal.

As we proceed in the actual planning process there are six principles that need to be kept in mind.

Present Choice

The principle of present choice teaches us that current decisions limit future action. What does this mean? Let us suppose that our missionary organization is about to go into a certain country or a certain province and the goal in this endeavor is church planting. As we become more definite we say that within five years we want churches started in the population centers. Within ten years, we will have a specific number of churches in these particular locations.

Now, we are agreed. We are entering this new area. There is mutual commitment that this is our goal, but after we get in there we find that these poor people do not know how to read and write. Are we going to have some literacy work? Then we find that these people are ill. Are we going to have some medical work? Then after awhile, we find that these people are hungry. They need some aid in agricultural development. Are we going to have some agricultural missionaries come in? Are we going to predetermine our goal in advance or are we to proliferate our activities after we are in, oftentimes to the weakening of all our purposes? What determines our goals? Is it need?

A missionary in children's work had a classic example of this problem. She was working alongside two or three couples in an area in Japan, and soon after she became involved in the children's work she found that in the wintertime all the children coming to the meetings had runny noses. So she would wipe their noses.Well, she found that all she was doing was wiping noses! Finally, she decided, "My goal is not to see that they have clean noses. My goal in these limited thirty or forty minutes that I have these children is to teach them something they will never forget from the Word of God." So she let their noses drip!

What determines what we are going to do? Necessity? Or are we going to make decisions now that will limit future action? This is why planning is difficult. Once we get into the thing we will find many other noble purposes which may or may not be of God. The fact that they are noble, the fact that they are needful activities, does not necessarily mean that we are qualified to get involved in them. Sometimes we proliferate our activities to the weakening of our main purposes. In planning we have to determine in advance.

Positive Action

The principle of positive action teaches us that the probability of a future event occurring increases as effort is applied systematically toward its realization. We have X number of people, X number of hours, and X amount of money. Our resources are limited, and we must not have them dissipated. This is why we must say, "We want a ditch dug from A to B" instead of, "All right. All of you as you feel led, dig the ditch."

We must have a goal commitment, a goal understanding, that forces us to be drawn together in its completion. I see this from the missionary's point of view and the pastor's point of view. This is a never-ending problem. The pastor or missionary says the job is church planting or evangelizing. Then he feels pressure to engage in a myriad of other activities, to the exclusion of the original purpose. The point is, we ought to be so oriented to the goal that we will critically evaluate these other pressing needs.

I find that most Christian organizations are so diversified in their activities that they are ineffective in everything. We have an exaggerated concept about our abilities and resources and an undisciplined approach to our task. One mission executive put down in his goals for his organization: "Our goal is to evangelize the whole world." What an exaggerated concept of his abilities and resources!

Commensurate Effort

The principle of commensurate effort teaches us that effort applied should be commensurate with or proportionate to the results desired. If we could just grasp that one thing, what a difference it could make in our ministry. But again, it presupposes an identified goal and a commitment to that goal. It critically looks at everything we are doing and says, "Here is the goal to which we are committed." But we are so subjective that we have great difficulty evaluating this sort of thing critically.

Planning Stability

The principle of planning stability teaches us that the stability of a plan tends to vary inversely with its extension. This means that I can plan very accurately for a week, with less accuracy for a month, with even less accuracy for a year, and with even less accuracy as the time is extended further. What does this mean in regard to planning? Does it mean that because of the instability of the lengthening of the plan, I should not plan? No, it makes planning all the more imperative. Also, it means that I will constantly update my plan. Planning is continuing work.

Potential Resistance

The greater the departure of planned changes from present ways, the greater the potential resistance by the people involved. Do you know who resists change? We resist change. And it is perhaps true that the older we are the more we resist it, but this is not necessarily true. The more insecure we are, the more we resist change. Provincialism contributes to resistance to change. We have to anticipate resistance to change and we cannot scold our people when they resist change. Some pastors I have talked to do not have a good word to say for their congregation in this area: "These people resist everything that is new and innovative." Let us appreciate the fact that we also resist change, that we do not want someone coming in and imposing something new on us. If we realize this about ourselves, it will help us to realize it about other people.

Future Events

Future events tend to result from current and past occurrences. Organizations are what they have been becoming. We determine tomorrow to the extent that we identify clearly what we want to accomplish and apply efforts today to bring it to pass. This is present diligence with clearly defined tomorrow mindedness.

5 Identify the Goals

The Establishing of Objectives

I am not concerned with what your objectives are, but I am concerned that you know what they are and that people with whom you work know what they are.

Now we turn our attention to one of the very important components of planning. In a previous chapter we defined the various components of planning, beginning with the work of estimating the future and going down through programs, policies, budgets, schedules, and so on. One of the most important aspects of planning, in fact, a component completely inseparable from the very concept of planning is the establishing of objectives. We must understand what our objectives are. We must be able to articulate them. They must be in written form. They must be widely displayed. People must have access to them. The people within our organization must be committed to them. In short, everyone in our organization must know what the objectives are.

What Is Our Purpose?

To a very large degree, the effectiveness of our corporate efforts in any human enterprise depends on our ability to concisely articulate our objectives, and the degree to which we are corporately enthusiastic about these objectives. In international organizations and operations, like missions, we get into all kinds of trouble. A frequent complaint I have heard from new missionaries and from older ones who can remember the frustrations of their earlier years is, "I am not doing what I came out here to do. I am not engaged in the kind of work that was described to me when I was in seminary." I know the arguments. But still there is this basic frustration. On the one hand we visualize our purposes as one thing and then when we get to our field of service we find that we are involved in something altogether different. At the point we rationalize: "Well, look, Olan, you've got to do what the Lord leads you to do."

The problem really is one of not knowing what our objectives are. Frequently when I talk to people from the same organization, I get two or more sets of answers for the same question. I am not concerned with what your objectives are, but I am concerned that you know what they are and that people with whom you work know what they are. I am concerned that everything possible be directed toward the accomplishing of those objectives, regardless of what they are.

I saw a very interesting article in a daily devotional magazine sometime ago. It speaks eloquently on this subject of objectives. A newly-hired traveling salesman wrote his first report to the home office. It stunned the executives in the sales department because it was obvious that the "new help" was a very poor speller and lacked a grasp of the fundamentals of English. This is what he wrote: "I seen this outfit which they never bought a dime's worth of nothin' from us and I sole them some goods. I am now going to Chicawgo." Before the services of the salesman could be terminated by the sales manager, this letter came from Chicago, "I cum here and sole them haff a millyon." Fearful if he did, and afraid if he did not fire the man, the sales manager dumped the problem in the lap of the president. The following morning the executives and office personnel were amazed to see a memo from the president posted on the bulletin board with the two letters written by the new salesman. It read like this: "We've ben spendin' two much time tryin' to spel instead of tryin' to sel. Let's watch those sails. I want everybody should read these letters from Gootch who is on the rode doin' a grate job for us and you should go out and do like he done." We should find out what we are supposed to do, and then do it.

One day I was showing a visitor around a church which had about 2,000 people in attendance. It was pastored by a friend of mine and had the oddest kind of arrangement you would ever want to see. I was showing this fellow around and explaining how this works and how that works. It is the most unconventional set-up, and my friend quickly spotted that and said, "Somebody ought to tell this pastor that this will not work." Well, the only problem was, it did work. This pastor was accomplishing his objectives.

Earlier I said that everything should be directed toward the accomplishment of our objectives. Organizational structure should lend itself relentlessly to the accomplishment of those objectives. Policies should contribute to the accomplishment of those objectives. Precedent and what we learn from history should dictate to us how to accomplish our objectives. But our problem most of the time is that we do not really know what our objectives are.

Objective Questions

Lorne Sanny, the successor to Dawson Trotman in the Navigator movement, is a sharp and creative manager. He was not always so. After his succession to the leadership, Lorne went through a very difficult period. It was only after he read a little booklet titled *Management,* written by the President of the National Bank of Detroit, that Lorne began to see that here were some skills he could acquire. After studying management for a number of years, Lorne Sanny framed four questions relative to objectives, because he found that he had to have some point of contact with the people who were serving under him. These were the most perceptive objective-oriented questions I have ever seen.

Lorne says, "There are four things I always ask people who report to me. First, I want to know plainly, *"What are your objectives?"* Start working on this and it will revolutionize your life. Ask this question about the next sermon you are going to preach. What are my objectives in delivering this sermon? What are my objectives in having this business meeting? What are my objectives in having this interview with this person?

Second, *What are your opportunities? What are your open doors?* Often opportunities can be made; often they cannot. We must be perceptive enough to know which doors are open. A lot of time can be wasted waiting idly for doors to open and energy can be wasted trying to open doors that simply can't be opened.

Third, *What are your resources?* Here we must be realistic, not mystical. Do not spiritualize where God demands a practical outlook. Do not become spiritually evasive where God demands pragmatism. What are my resources? How many people do I have? How many hours do I have? How much money do I have? How many cars do

I have? How many Bibles do I have? How much literature do I have?

The fourth question has to do with strategy and then it also reviews the list from the bottom to the top. *What is your strategy for applying your resources to your opportunities to obtain your objectives?* This will force a person to think creatively. This removes the responsibility from the manager to devise all the steps to be taken, and thrusts the creative responsibility on the individuals themselves.

The Power of Goals

Objectives clearly articulated and mutually agreed on in a group have a powerful effect. This concept more than anything else explains the supreme accomplishments of new organizations that accomplish a great deal in a short period of time. Probably some of you reminisce about the old days of your church or organization when you accomplished so much. Of course, we tend to distort the past. We tend to remember only the good about the past and forget the bad. Someone has said: "There are only two good places to be: the place where you have just been and the place where you are going." We normally can look realistically only at the moment, but nonetheless it is a fact that new organizations are highly goal-oriented or objective-oriented and everything is subservient to the goal.

This need not be exclusively a characteristic of the new or recently-emerged organization. It can be a continuing characteristic of any organization if we want it to be and if we are willing to make it so at all costs.

Let us see the powerful effect of clear objectives. Most good work in management is problem-oriented; that is, it aims at accomplishing some specific end, some goal, or it aims at achieving some terminal point. The definition of these objectives for the whole organization, for all subordinate organizations, and for individuals in it, is the logical starting place for management improvement. This is important. Many old, staid, ponderous, slow-moving churches and Christian organizations can be rejuvenated to a goal orientation. Many cannot. If it is possible, then it is so only as we make an attack on this subject of objectives. Every book you read on the subject of management says the same thing. This is where we have to start: the objectives for the total organization. Put this in a pyramid form. The top piece would be the objective of the total organization. Everything underneath this, every subordinate organization, must likewise be committed in this direction, though it will have goals all its own. This applies to the individual also. Every individual within this organization must have goals that are incorporated into the main objectives.

Four Effects of Unclear Objectives

1. Unclear objectives lead to unclear methods of operation. The absence of a goal justifies almost any activity espoused by an individual under the guise of, "This is my burden," or "This is my calling," or "This is the Lord's leading." I do not mean to minimize this nor speak lightly of holy things. But I think there is more evasiveness in these pronouncements than most of us in Christian work are willing to admit, and it is tragic. If you do not have a goal, then any road will get you there.
2. Results cannot be measured without some prior expectation against which to judge them. In other words, if we do not have clear objectives, then almost any level or degree or quality of performance will satisfy the people involved. Almost any activity can be justified on an individualistic basis. This is where we are in missions and in our churches.

    There are, however, some people who will never work in an organization. If we were able to devise an ideal organization, some people would never fit into it. Accommodate these people outside organizational structures. Recognize that not everyone can conform to an organizational structure. If there are individuals who must work on their own, let them go! The great bulk of humanity, however, needs the kind of restraint and control provided by an organization.

3. If we are not clear on our objectives, we do not know when things are drifting. One does not realize it until a lifetime has been spent and then, suddenly it dawns, "I didn't achieve it. I didn't hit it." Oh, we rationalize, we exonerate ourselves, we excuse ourselves, we make allowances; but in the end we find we have failed.

4. People in an organization cannot perform with maximum effectiveness if they are unaware of the goals, the purposes of their work, or how well they are doing in relation to the goals.

There are three main problems in managing workers. They are (1) uncertainty of the job, (2) how am I doing, and (3) where do I go for help? I have talked with scores of missionaries who have spent a term on the field and have not known how they were doing until they were ready to go home and had a prefurlough interview! One reason we fail to tell people how they are doing is that some of us in responsible positions are insecure ourselves. We have not trusted the Holy Spirit to give us the courage to face a person and tell how he or she is doing. People want help. They need help. If we want to have effective management results we will build into our situations ways for people to get help.

"Look, I'm having trouble with my wife and children. Where do I go for help?

"I'm having problems with the local or national church. Where do I go for help?"

"I'm having problems in my own mind with some theological questions. Where do I get help? Is there a person or a group to which I can go for help?"

A good manager will establish a relationship with people so that they will gladly come and say, "I need help. Can you tell me what to do?"

In articulating these goals, we prepare a very basic foundation for all of our future performance. Goals are not always adhered to with equal enthusiasm by every member of the organization. People deeply committed come in but they become disillusioned and need to be reminded repeatedly of the goals of the organization. We must be reoriented to the goal week after week, year after year.

Establishing Goals

Now the question comes: "How do I establish goals?" First of all, there are two types of goals, long-range and short-range. Long-range goals usually run five years or more. Anything less than that becomes short-range. How are these goals established? This is the hardest work you will ever do. It is easy to write down what you think ought to be done. However, when twenty, thirty, fifty or a hundred people are involved it becomes difficult. Start with the ultimate goal. What do you want to accomplish ultimately? For example, this could be to build cathedrals in every metropolitan center in Africa. Determine what the goal is and then work back toward "today." That is the big job.

When obstacles arise, you may be tempted to avoid them, and concentrate on other goals, perhaps an intermediate-range goal. Management is concerned with applying the pressure to get back on course, again heading for the target. You know how missiles work. The basic function of the guidance system of a rocket is first of all to determine the goal or the target, and then to feed back to the earth at a guidance center or computer the detailed, minute information that will tell the programmer if the rocket is veering off the slightest bit. In other words, the operator does not wait to correct the rocket; he reacts instantly. The missile must be pushed back on course.

That is the concern of management; not with dominating another human personality, nor with asserting itself, nor with acquiring and attaining status. Management is concerned with objectives. This is why you must use management skills.

What happens when you do not use management skills? You veer off the course. Not only that, if you do not use management control, when you veer off, confusion, loss of confidence, and frustration results.

Lack of Management Brings Frustration

The one emotion I observe most in Christian work is frustration. Not because people fail to respond to the gospel (any biblically-oriented person has an answer to that kind of devilish frustration), but frustration results from a lack of management within our human enterprise. I have been in countries where the missionaries are suffering all sorts of hardships. In southeast Asia, Thailand, Viet Nam, and Cambodia missionaries live in tremendously primitive situations. I have seen national pastors working in situations in Cambodia, where they could not hand out a piece of literature without a permit from a police officer. I have known of pastors who have had their wives imprisoned because they allegedly gave out a piece of literature without permission. These pastors have been absolutely radiant in the face of that kind of persecution. These situations do not cause frustration. Yet in the face of poor management missionaries have been in absolute bondage and defeat. This could be avoided if we simply recognized some management skills and acquired them.

Rules for Establishing Objectives

Someone has said that there are five rules for establishing objectives. The first is, *consider past performance.* Know precisely what has been the situation in the past. Records, trends, and honest input from your followers provide this background. Second, *set realistic levels.* It is very easy for religious workers to violate this under the guise of faith! Third, *use measurable terms.* This is easiest in relation to income, attendance, concerts, and facilities. It is enormously difficult in areas like learning attitudes and morale. Fourth, *build in an improvement factor.* People will not long pursue mere ideals that have no rewards. And few rewards have the dynamics of improvement. Fifth, *take people action.* To secure the creative cooperation of followers, a leader must provide for participation on their part. This does not imply allowing them to vote; but it does involve participation.

Group Goals vs. Individual Goals

Another aspect that should be mentioned is the difference between corporate goals (the total goal of the association of human beings) and individual goals. There is a distinction. We cannot adequately determine individual goals until we have determined corporate goals. There must be the same relationship between corporate goals and individual goals that there is between long-range and short-range goals. Start with long-range goals and work back. Likewise, start with corporate goals and then begin to work in departmental goals, divisional goals, project goals, institutional goals, and individual goals (see pyramid diagram).

Within the pyramid there may be other pyramids. If the goal is the planting of churches in cities in hitherto unreached areas, there may be a large project, e.g., a housing development, and within this you would have another pyramid. Within that pyramid there could be other pyramids, depending on how large this organization is. Individuals would be related in these situations as well as in the overall picture. All of these activities move toward the ultimate goal. It is this concept that makes the difference between success and failure. A strong natural leader instinctively, by virtue of dynamic personality, accomplishes this sort of thing. In a very natural way, almost totally psychological, he or she achieves the goal very effectively. But in the absence of such a person, articulation of objectives and adherence to those objectives can do the same thing.

The difference between long-range and short-range goals, between corporate and individual goals, must be clear. Therefore, the prime target is the determination of objectives. What is the group trying to accomplish? Assuming that objectives have been established, people action has satisfactorily been taken, and people are committed to the stated goals, the next thing to do is to organize for a particular function.

Pyramid Within a Pyramid
One, two and three make up A, then
person 2 along with subordinates make up team B.
Person 2 becomes the link between the two teams.

6 Learn the Basics

Management Organizing Principles

The criterion by which we measure organizational normality is the achievement of goals. Briefly and succinctly, the implications of organizational dynamics are growth, development, and maturity.

In a recent issue of *U.S. News and World Report* there was an interesting story about a British military team trying to cut down on the manpower used in handling a field cannon. Six men had been assigned to each cannon but there were only five jobs. The men studied each job as described in the instruction manual. From the first edition on, every manual called for a crew of six. Finally, they located the man who had originally written the manual, a retired general. They asked him what the sixth man was supposed to do. He replied, "The sixth man? He holds the horses." Horses had not been used for many, many years, but the job persisted. No reason was necessary; precedent had become reason enough!

If our objective is clearly defined and if we are convinced that it is of God and we are committed to it, the people involved in the organization will accept it as God's assignment. Then it is necessary to devise an organizational structure which contributes to achieving the objectives.

A Definition of Organizing

Management organizing is the *grouping, arranging, and relating of the work to be performed by a group of people to accomplish the goal effectively.* The little blocks in the typical organizational chart do not represent status nor salary levels but merely identify and relate work which is necessary to accomplish organizational goals.

A manager must develop an organization capable of accomplishing its objectives. Often alteration of the structure becomes necessary. What things might happen which would indicate the need for alteration? A change of goal, or the capacities of the people involved, or the environment in which the goal is being accomplished might signal a need to alter objectives. Fifty years ago in the United States, Sunday evening services were very popular as a way to reach the unconverted. People often did not have anywhere else to go, so they went to church on Sunday night. They did not attend on Sunday morning because they slept in. They did not have television to watch nor have as many cars then as they do now. But things have changed. If we get any unconverted people into a church today, it is on Sunday morning, certainly not on Sunday night. Yet many churches doggedly persist on having a Sunday evening evangelistic service. We refuse to accept the changes dictated by an evolution in our environment. We have task and tradition orientation!

Alvin Brown says, "Organization defines the part which each member of an enterprise is expected to perform and the relations between such members to the end that their concerted effort or endeavor shall be most effective for the purpose of the enterprise."

Mooney and Riley describe organization as "the form of every human association for the attainment of a common purpose."

General Foods Corporation defines organization as, "the plan by which a group of people pool their efforts toward designated objectives though definition and division of activities, responsibilities, and authority." Why do we give a person a specific job, give specific authority, and allow freedom to make specific kinds of decisions? Because that is the best way to accomplish the goal!

The Implication of Organizational Dynamics

The simple fact is that organizations are made up of people. People change, environments change, the demands on an organization are constantly changing. This means that the people within the organization must be willing to have their structure and activities altered to accomplish the goal. The organization, like a human being, must develop.

Organizations may be brought into existence, operate effectively for a short time, only to stagnate and degenerate as their environment moves on ahead of them. They just stay bogged down and entangled and do not develop. Organizations must live and breathe, evolve, grow, and change, or their lifetime is predictably shortened.

In the physical development of a person the criterion by which we measure normality is the relationship of that individual to others. The criterion by which we measure organizational normality is the achievement of goals.

Briefly and succinctly, the implications of organizational dynamics are growth, development, and maturity.

Purpose vs. Sentimentality

There must be purpose versus sentiment in Christian organizations. In the business world not all businesses are successful and well organized. It is amazing how many people study business management but never use that knowledge. However, business has one advantage that we do not have in Christian work; it has a profit and loss statement. If a business does not show a profit, and over a long period continues to show a loss, somebody complains—usually the stockholders. Why? They want a return on their investment. Not only do they want a return on their investment, they also want protection for their capital and the greatest protection of that capital is the continuing functioning of that organization. Stockholders want to make money on the money they have invested. If they do not see this happening, they complain loudly. But unfortunately, we do not have this set-up in Christian work.

We can sink into unbelievable organizational ineffectiveness in Christian work and few supporters will say anything. If complaints are made, they are not spoken loudly, or somebody cries, "Oh, you're touching the Lord's anointed," or, "You're fighting against God," or, "Didn't God bring this organization into existence?" That is sad. Those statements do not make much sense, but we say them anyway. What is it then that perpetuates the organization? It is sentiment.

One time we had a very serious situation in a church I was serving. A well-meaning but sticky sentimentalist said in a deacon's meeting one night when we were discussing the problem, "Friends, my advice is not to touch the situation. Let's maintain peace." Well, there is a time when silence is not golden: it is yellow cowardice. There is a time when we must sweep aside this kind of peacefulness and sentimentality to accomplish our objectives. Do you know that in church, purposefulness is always considered eccentric, always kind of coming at the status quo from the flank? And yet, it is this kind of purposefulness to which God has called us. But we often find that we prefer to perpetuate the form on the basis of sentiment rather than to insist on accomplishing our purpose.

Some of us may be so bogged down in sentiment that our church or organization does not have a chance for renewal and adaptation. If that is the case, it is tragic! Our donors or church members do not help. They feed the evil root of sentimentality rather than holding us to the highest and saying: "Are you sure that what you are doing is essential? Can you justify your being there?" Your members will not say that. They will pat you on the head and give you another love offering. An awesome responsibility rests on us to evaluate ourselves and develop a goal orientation.

You probably have noticed on the management outline (page 26) that under the four major functions of management according to Allen are listed all of the activities that apply to those major headings. For example, under management organizing are the activities of organizing; also, the developing of the structure, the maintaining of relationships, and delegation. Let us look at some management organizing principles which relate to organizing as a whole, to the developing of the structure, to the work of delegation, and to the work of establishing and maintaining relationships.

1. *The objective.* The organizational structure should be designed to accomplish established objectives. It follows from this that when the organizational structure no longer accomplishes objectives, discard it, alter it, or subject it to whatever is necessary to accomplish the objectives.
2. *Specialization.* The work assigned to individuals should be specialized insofar as it is consistent

with effective human effort. This is the genius of the assembly line. Specialization applies not only to assembly line situations but to managerial situations as well. The more specialized we can make the work, the more skilled the person is apt to become in that work, and the more effective he or she is apt to be over a lengthy period.

Some time ago I was consulted regarding a situation where a woman was assigned to counseling and to bookkeeping. You cannot imagine two more opposite types of work. The woman was terribly frustrated because she was at an age in her life when she was concerned about her own accomplishments. Usually, people at about forty tend to panic. "What have I done? What am I achieving?" Between the ages of forty and forty-five, people often make drastic changes in their vocations under the panic pressure of accomplishment. Her problem was that she was not excelling in either field. With a bit of pressure she was relieved of the bookkeeping and moved into counseling (which she preferred), and she developed an attitude which was much more wholesome.

3. *Management emphasis.* When called on to supervise two or more differing types of work, a manager tends to show preferential emphasis in decisions and choices. These preferences will be determined primarily by previous relationships or activities. This can be good or bad, depending on the needs of the situation.

4. *Maximum span.* A manager should oversee the maximum number of people he or she can effectively manage. This is assuming that we view management as a type of work to be performed and we recognize it as a legitimate assignment. The number depends on a variety of things, the most important of which is the capacity of the manager. Some

people have a greater capacity than others. The number depends also on the type of work the people are doing. One can obviously oversee more ditch-diggers than research scientists. In the third place, the number depends on location and/or dispersal of personnel.

I was involved in a situation where one man was responsible for eighteen men located across the United States and Canada. This is an impossible situation. There are not enough days in the week, there are not enough planes flying, and if there were, one person does not have the energy to relate to that many men spread over that wide an area. So it depends on capacity; the type of work; and location or the dispersal of the people who are being supervised. However, all of that being considered, the manager should manage as many people as he or she effectively can.

5. *Minimum levels*. The number of organizational levels should be kept at a minimum. Proliferating the organizational levels will not necessarily increase the effectiveness of the organization itself. Minimize those levels. The more levels multiplied this way, the more difficulties are created.The reason is obvious. It takes time for information and decisions to go from the top to the bottom.

Incidentally, have you ever noticed the instinctive answer to every problem? The problem posed is: "We are not getting the work done that we should." The first answer, the easiest answer, the spontaneous answer is, "Let us get more people." *More people does not insure the accomplishment of more work.* It only insures the presence of more people. Sometimes work simplification is the answer, not an increased staff.

6. *Carry-over*. The early characteristics of organization tend to persist in later organizational forms.

To put it simply, "You never outlive your past." Some of these earlier characteristics will follow you to the very end. You can make appreciable changes, but the past carries over.

7. *Control limits.* Delegation should proceed only to the limit of effective control. Just as a person can only do so much, so a person can be accountable for only so much.

8. *Commensurate authority.* Authority should be delegated commensurate with responsibility.

9. *Complete accountability.* The superior is always accountable for the actions of subordinates. It is not a very pleasant position, but it is always a necessary position.

10. *Single reporting relationships.* Each person should be accountable to only one supervisor.

Ten Commandments of Good Organization

There are two kinds of efficiency. One kind is apparent and is produced in organizations only through the exercise of mere discipline. This is but an imitation of the second, or true efficiency which springs, as Woodrow Wilson said, from "the spontaneous cooperation of a free people." If you are a manager, no matter how great or small your responsibility, it is your job to create and develop this voluntary cooperation among the people whom you supervise. For no matter how powerful a combination of money, machines, and materials an organization may have, they are dead and sterile without a team of *willing, thinking,* and *articulate* people to guide them.

Here are "Ten Commandments of Good Organization," I have slightly adapted from the American Management Association.

1. Definite and clear-cut responsibilities should be assigned to each person or position. We might

know today what our job is, but the situation might change so that tomorrow we do not know. We need adequate supervision so that we can rediscover what our job is when it has evolved.

2. Responsibility should always be coupled with corresponding authority.

3. No change should be made in the scope or responsibilities of a position without a definite understanding to that effect on the part of all persons concerned.

4. No executive or employee, occupying a single position in the organization, should be subject to orders from more than one source. Every person should have only one boss. Where it is necessary for one person to have two or three positions, there should not only be a clear understanding as to who gives orders with respect to which work, and the time allocation for these positions. Otherwise, the individual is going to be torn and subordinates may well be frustrated because they take orders from so many people.

5. Orders should never be given to subordinates over the head of a responsible executive. The manager tells the supervisor what a certain subordinate under the supervisor should do; the manager does not go directly to the subordinate.

6. Criticisms of subordinates should be made privately, and in no case should a subordinate be criticized in the presence of executives or employees of equal or lower rank.

7. No dispute or difference between executive or employee as to authority or responsibilities should be considered too trivial for prompt and careful attention.

8. Promotions, wage changes, and disciplinary action should always be approved by the executive immediately superior to the one directly responsible.

9. No executive or employee should ever be required, or expected, to be at the same time an assistant to, and a critic of, another.

10. Executives whose work is subject to regular inspection should, whenever practicable, be given the assistance and facilities necessary to enable them to maintain an independent check of the quality of their own work. The truth is that we are harder on ourselves than our superiors would be. Executives should be given opportunity to report to you so that there can be not only your appraisal of their work but also their own appraisals of their work, both coming from the same standard.

Sources of Authority

Look at four sources of authority by which an individual manages.

Authority of competence. The more competent the subordinates know you are, the more confident they will be that you know what you are talking about. And, the more likely they will be to follow your orders, requests, and suggestions. This does not mean that you can manage a treasurer or bookkeeper only if you yourself are an expert treasurer or bookkeeper. It implies your competency as a manager in general.

Authority of position. This gives you the right to tell someone else what to do. This has teeth. If you are elected chairman or director, you have to fill your position. What are the two greatest enemies of leadership? To like and to want to be liked. "I cannot discipline this fellow—I like him. I cannot be too hard on that woman—I want her to like me."

My father was a construction worker for the International Paper Company from the time he was nineteen years old until his death. Sometime ago he was building the largest paper mill in the world at Vicksburg, Mississippi. I was visiting there and he was showing me through the new mill. We were riding along in the car, and I said, "Dad, what do your men think of you?"

Dad said, "Huh, I can't talk that way to you; you're a preacher."

I said, "No, I'm really interested. What do your men think about you?"

He puffed on his cigar, looked at me, and sort of grinned and said, "Well, I heard a couple of men talking in the room next to me the other day. They didn't know I was in there and one of them said, 'Hendrix? Why that grey-headed old...!'"

Dad sucked on his cigar vigorously, and said, "I don't care what they think about me. My job is to build mills, not to make friends."

I thought, "Give me that kind of courage too." Not that ruthlessness but that kind of commitment to a purpose. If you are a "peace at any price" kind of person, you are going to be a poor manager.

Authority of your personality. The easier it is for other people to talk to you, to listen to you, or to work with you, the easier they will find it to respond to your wishes. On the one hand, authoritatively fill your position; on the other hand, be as human as you can possibly be. Position and personality are the two sides of the same coin.

Authority of character. This component is your credit rating with other people, that is, your reliability, honesty, loyalty, sincerity, and your personal morals and ethics. In the Philippines somebody said to me, "Mr. So and So? Oh, he is one of the outstanding preachers in the Republic of the Philippines, but I would not work with that man for anything. You cannot trust him. He will tell you one thing and tell somebody else on the staff just the opposite." No character, no integrity, no reliability, no trustworthiness! We manage by the authority of our character.

7 Understand Your Group

The Two Basic Groups

In some of our minds, the Church exists to perpetuate its existence. The Church should exist to accomplish the goals its Lord has put before it.

Let's move on to an analysis of the two basic groups or mentalities that prevail in the extremes of group situations.

The Centric Group

The centric group is an association of people—religious, educational, social, or industrial—in which the general level of personal concern is greater than the general level of group concern. The result is an introspection, a turning in on the group itself.

With the centric group there is an incompatibility of objectives. Where there is an ingrown aspect, the people involved tend to give primacy to their own objectives rather than to the objectives of the group. Not only that, there is resistance to authority in the centric group.The centric group is generally control-oriented. Everyone is demanding to be heard. The centric group gives primary consideration to this question: "Are we structured so that everyone can have his say?"

I am not advocating any form of government. Every form of government can degenerate into a centric group and any form of government can be a goal-oriented group. There is a resistance to authority in the centric group. While this group is always centered in itself, it is never looking critically at performance but always looking critically at control. "Are we giving everyone a right to say all that he or she feels?"

A mission organization that is centric in its association and functions from a group point of view is generally made up of mature people. Alone they are spiritually responsible, imaginative, poised, and disciplined. But in a group situation all of these aspects of the centric group come to the fore. Why? I do not understand it, but I know that there is something about an association of people on certain topics that tends toward the centric aspect. Generally it is government, and it revolves around a question of decision making or authority.

The Radic Group

In *the radic group* the level of group concern is greater than the general level of personal concern.

In discussing the centric and radic groups do not assume that one is secular and the other is sacred. That is not necessarily true. Some of the most radic groups I know are utterly secular, for example, the U.S. Peace

Corps. A lot of the humanitarian enterprises of the world are radic. The radic group tends to radiate out rather than turn in. This group has goal-orientation and perceptive team work. Jesus Christ designed this type of group in both the apostolate and in the Church in its growth and development.

The Church was always to be a radic group, and it is a sign of degeneracy when we become centric. In some of our minds, the Church exists to perpetuate its existence. The Church should exist to accomplish the goals its Lord has put before it. Quite a difference! Do we exist to perpetuate our existence? That is centric. Do we exist to accomplish our Lord's goal? That is radic. Generally a group starts out radic and degenerates to centric. The extent to which we have become centric is the extent to which we have passed down the line through a work-orientation or a task-orientation to the bitter dregs of a control-orientation.

Management is not teaching somebody else something. Management is assimilating knowledge and beginning to demonstrate it and infecting people with it. Our strategy must be "What can I learn to demonstrate in my managerial post that will become central in its growth?" not, "What can I teach this person in order to set him right?" Centric groups do not grow appreciably. Centric groups tend to stagnate, if not in the assimilation of new personnel, at least in the dynamics of their activity. Particularly is this true in religion because in religious types of work, we must attract people. Centric groups simply stop being attractive.

The chief danger for the radic group is becoming so fragmented in its purposes that different groups and different individuals have different purposes and they begin to compete. This will always lead to a centric orientation. It is not that any group is solidly radic. One aspect or the other tends to dominate.

Does the goal still grip us? Is it still worthy of our commitment? The danger here is to have one thing in writing and another thing in practice—a Jekyll and Hyde management practice.

It is much easier to train a group to function in accordance with a predescribed plan of conformity than it is to train a group to achieve a goal. I may say to my boy, "Now do this. No, you may not do that. Yes, do that. That's fine." Giving instructions is easier than saying, "Now, look, young man, you are to conduct yourself in an honorable, upright way so that at the end of your life you will be able to say, 'I have lived honorably and decently.' "

The Importance of the Goal

What holds the radic group together? It is the goal. The more we are obsessed with the goal, the more we are willing to tolerate individual differences within the organization. The less we are obsessed with the goal, the more we need to have personality conformity within the organization. Somebody comes to you and he does not say things just the way you would say them. If we are goal-oriented we say, "This man has something to contribute and we will endure much from him because he is going to help us reach our goal." The breadth of tolerance in the radic group is much greater than the breadth of tolerance in the centric group. A strong goal-oriented mission will tend to reproduce a strong goal-oriented church and a strong goal-oriented young people's movement within that church. The same principle applies. You have to start where you are with your group. You cannot walk into another group, one in which you are not responsible for leadership and direction, and say, "Here's how this ought to be done."

Single-Person Rule and Team Rule

There are two basic types of organizational structure. These are single-person rule and team rule.

Generally, religious organizations come into existence and function best initially as a single-person rule. The woman with the burden gets the job. The man with the vision makes a decision. He is the person who has attracted people around him and initiates a one-person rule. A dictatorship, whether it is in a religious environment or in a political situation, is always the most efficient form of government. If you have a benevolent dictator, you are in business. The problem is that dictators tend to become self-centered—even in religious situations. The issue here is decision making. Who decides what this person is going to do? How much money is she going to spend? Where are they going to work? Which house are they going to live in?

The alternative to this one person making all the decisions is team work, multiple-person rule. I do not mean that the alternative to one individual making all the decisions is everybody making the decisions. That is compounding the red tape which must be gone through to arrive at a decision. But the other alternative to one person deciding everything is to let everybody make the decisions they can in keeping with the information they have at hand and the competency they possess. In other words, decisions should always be pushed down the organizational chart. If you must err, err in asking a person to make too many decisions rather than in not asking for enough.

Decisions should be made on the lowest possible level, as near as possible to where the work is actually performed. Unless a one-person ruler is tremendously goal-oriented, that person will make as many decisions as he or she possibly can. Even pastors, unless goal-oriented, will grasp for as much decision making as possible. Why? To protect themselves and to be more comfortable. The only alternative I know of to insure that this person will constantly push decisions down is goal-orientation. Otherwise, our very nature will cause us to accumulate decisions at the top. This retards the progress of the whole group by forcing everything to be channeled through one individual. But what does this do to the goal? We achieve goals best when people are allowed to make as many decisions as possible which affect their work. Let your aim be to push decision-making down the structure.

If the group is not committed to the goal, you may as well fall back and regroup. This assumes that a leader is constantly going to be training people how to make decisions.

A man who reports to me came in some time ago. He had a thorny situation and he said, "What shall I do?"

"Let's discuss the facts," I said.

He laid the whole thing out before me, and I made some observations and asked some questions. We talked for some time about the problem.

"All right," he said, "What do you want me to do?"

I said, "This is your decision. I want you to make the decision. What do *you* want to do about it?"

It was important enough that I felt I had to know what the decision was, but he made the decision. I did not precisely agree. There were a couple of things I thought should be different, but they were not big enough for me to say, "Change that." I let him make his decision. That man grew a foot taller. If I had thought his decision was radically wrong, I would have explained why and I would have asked him to reconsider it. Any leader who cannot train decision-making capacities in subordinates is not worthy of being in a managerial position! The person at the top must make decisions that are major, that affect the overall situation or interpretation of policy.

There was a general in World War II whose fellow commanding officers got together and said, "We think such and such an attack ought to be made." The general said, "No, it won't work. We will lose too many men. Here is why it will not work." They considered. They overrode this man who had to command his own men. They said, "Our decision is, we attack this way." He said, "I disagree. These are my men, and we are going to lose."

They replied, "This is what we're going to do anyway."
He yielded and sure enough his predictions were right. He
lost many men. His own subordinate officers came back
and asked, "Why?" The general said, "Our decision
was . . ." and he never once indicated that he had differed.

It is the absence of this kind of courage that causes
friction in churches and mission groups. If you do not
agree with what "they" say, are you going to go along?
What alternative do you have? The alternative is to split
the group and set "your" people at variance with one
another. You can create your own little domain if that is
what you want, or you can get out. The stronger the goal-
orientation, the stronger a leader will strive for cohesive-
ness. The less the goal-orientation, the more content a
leader will be to develop his own little domain. How do
you build courage? I really do not know except to develop
it yourself and hope it will rub off on the person who is
watching you. I think the more important the goal is to
you, the more courageous you will be to try to achieve it.

We must make a distinction. If a man comes to me and
says, "I want to talk to you personally and confidentially," that is no problem. But if he wants to talk to me
personally and confidentially about the work, there can
be no such thing as a personal and confidential conversa-
tion because it involves others. If it is a problem in his
own life and his own family situation, that is personal.
But if it involves a group goal, it is no longer personal. Tell
people everything you can and you will seldom be called
on to tell them things you should not. If they know you
are open and not secretive, they will not suspect you of
withholding information.

8 Share the Task

Delegation and Job Descriptions

A job description helps us know what our tasks are and why we are in the organization. A job description helps our boss to know what we are doing. It helps us to know what he or she expects of us, and it lets people around us know what we are doing. Likewise we know why their jobs exist.

What Is Delegation?

Delegation is one of the activities under the heading of Management Organizing. There are three components. But first, what do we mean by delegation? In a recent book, *The Effective Executive*, Peter Drucker listed three diagnostic questions for the effective managing of time.

When Drucker first got into management consulting, he realized that he had to have some way of quickly sizing up an organization, what it was doing, what it was like, and what its needs were.

1. What am I doing that really does not need to be done by me or anyone else?
2. Which of the activities on my time log could be handled as well, if not better, by someone else?
3. What do I do that wastes the time of other people?

Amplifying on these three points, Drucker went on to say that he discovered that a well-managed plant, office, business, organization is always dull-DULL! The recurrent crisis is by far the most common symptom of poor management. I think he is right.

Many attempts have been made to define delegation. One, for example, says, "Delegation is giving others the right to make your decisions." Another says "Delegation is to give authority to accompany responsibility." "Delegation is having other people do part of your work" is still another. I think all of these are inadequate. I would like us to agree on L. A. Allen's definition that, "Delegation is entrusting responsibility and authority and establishing lines of accountability."

Delegation is learning how to identify the work that we are doing and devising methods of passing these pieces of work on to other people, but maintaining a management check on these activities.

One of our Japanese pastors came to me and said, "Mr. Hendrix, I would like to ask you a question." I braced myself. He said, "There is an old Japanese proverb and I want to ask you if you think this proverb is true and accurate. It goes this way: 'A wise prince or lord knows even how many ashes are in the stove in the kitchen.' Is this a good proverb?" I tried to figure out what he was getting at and answered, "No, that is not a good proverb. A wise prince or lord does not necessarily know how many ashes there are in the stove, but he knows he has someone who does know how many ashes are in the kitchen stove." The pastor smiled. I am afraid I gave him some ammunition against some of my colleagues. Not that he needed it—I think he had enough of his own.

The Need for Delegation

Why should we consider delegation? Here are some reasons:

1. *You are not doing the big jobs that need to be done.* That is your job as the top executive. Someone says, "Communications have broken down in our church." Someone else says, "I don't know what my job is." That is your job, to help them find out what their job is. Demoralization has set in. Your job is to work on that. If you are not doing these big jobs that need to be done, you should consider delegation.

2. *You are missing deadlines.* One day I sat down with Clarence Jones before I made my first trip overseas and I said, "Clarence, you are a veteran, traveling everywhere, teaching people and lecturing on various subjects. Give me some guidelines. Tell me what to do and what not to do as I make this trip." He said, "Well, it is important to work on other people's time clock. Do not take your own American time clock."

   I have tried to do this and I know that deadlines are not as important in some cultures as they are in others. I know, for example, that in Japan the more important a letter is, the more time you give to contemplation before you answer it. An immediate response, instead of being the epitome of efficiency, is the representation of laxity and unconcern. I know that about Japan. However, where deadlines are set, you should meet them. Sometimes you are caught in cross-cultural situations where to miss deadlines is to create demoralization in a staff. If you are missing deadlines, if you are backlogged so that you cannot get things done when they are supposed to be done, you need to consider delegation.

3. *You now spend time on trivial tasks that others could do.* Here, we often face a problem of false modesty when we say, "Well, I'm not too good. I can't do that." We come to our service for Jesus Christ, recognizing that there are some things which we will do that no one else is eager to do. But we must not let trivial tasks force us into a corner, particularly when all they do is feed our own ego and our estimation of how humble we are.

4. *You have people who, if trained, could handle the job better than you.* One of our biggest problems in Christian work is our failure to properly appraise the potentialities of the people with whom we work. Having done so honestly, we serve both the individual and the organization well when we pass on challenging and rewarding tasks to others.

5. *You have an imbalance in the work load of your personnel.* Some individuals are underworked and others are overworked. You must help the overloaded to learn to delegate for themselves. One of the hardest things in the world is to teach people to look always at their work with the view, "Who can I get to do this so that I can give myself to a more important task?" We allow things that we do ourselves to become boss-imposed and system-imposed activities, instead of pushing them out and seeing that other people get them done. But often it is easier, and more comfortable when we do it ourselves. That is reverting to operating instead of managing.

6. *You have individuals who need new worlds to conquer.* They need new spheres of responsibility. People need to grow. A frequent reason given for leaving an organization is the feeling that there is nowhere left to go.

The Ethics of Delegation

For a long time I encountered all kinds of resistance when I talked about delegation, and I could not understand it. Why do Christian workers fight the concept of delegation? Finally, one man said to me, "How can I give someone else the right, authority, and assignment to do what God has called *me* to do?" I realized this was an ethical problem. This problem is very real and I do not minimize it. If God has called me to do something, then I cannot easily or lightly turn away from that and let somebody else take it up.

But I think this ethical problem is answered completely by going back again to the three ingredients of delegation, principally emphasizing accountability. Although I have delegated a piece of work, I retain ultimately the responsibility for its performance. Many times people have demonstrated to me their frustration because they gave somebody something to do and then, at the last minute, they discovered that it had not been done. Who is responsible? In the final analysis, those who delegated are responsible. I think this answers, then, the ethical question that comes with regard to delegation. If I give somebody else a job to do and have an understanding that they are going to do it, I cannot just turn my back and walk away from it. I am still responsible, and if it does not get done I have to answer for it. Mr. Harry Truman in his Presidential office used to have a sign worth remembering, "The buck stops here." Every manager ought to have that mentality. I am responsible and from this office there is no "passing the buck!" If the person did not do it, it is my fault.

Henry Brandt says, "People do what we *inspect* not what we *expect*." And it simply means that you have to solemnly and relentlessly inspect and establish lines for accountability. You have to accept that the person you have may not be able to follow through on a given assignment unless you continually supervise and check back and give concern, help and direction. To me, this answers the ethical question.

We are always in a state of conflict concerning what we would like to do and what we are gifted to do. People who have been in the ministry fifty years are still struggling with it. I do not have an easy answer, but I have developed some answers that satisfy me. I have decided never to desire to do anything that requires gifts my brethren do not recognize in me. I am not an individualist. I am a member of the body, a part of the organization. I will continually accept that I tend to have exaggerated notions of my abilities.

Resistance to Delegation

There are some barriers to delegation. Why is it that delegation is so difficult? Here are some reasons for resistance to delegation:

1. There is a reluctance to admit limitation. We don't like to admit that we can't easily do something. There are always people who are willing to take real responsibility for some segment of the work if the other person is willing to let go. The biggest problem is getting the person at the top to let go.
2. Tradition, desire for prestige, and desire to retain control contribute to resistance to delegation.
3. Lack of confidence in your staff. The more insecure we are, the more we tend to look with disdain on the capacity of the people around us because, we think, that makes us look better or bigger. Why is this? I am not sure that I know the reason, but we ought to be *the* people of all people who are poised and confident. Is it that we are possessive of our positions and defensive of our organizations and have only a minimum of goal commitment?
4. We doubt our ability to train someone else to do it our way. Many times our appraisal is on the basis of "how" something is done, not "whether" it is done.

5. Ignorance—some of us have never seen a particular assignment done properly.

To summarize, we have said that all of the reasons for people resisting delegation are within them, not outside them. All the reasons for resisting delegation are emotional. It is something within us that blocks us, not something from without.

Job Descriptions

The subject of job description relates dynamically and vitally to the entire plan, lead, organize, control concept. Look again at the outline and relate the subject of job descriptions to it. There are two places where job descriptions might be considered. Louis Allen inserts job descriptions into the subject of establishing objectives. Job descriptions can be there or under the subject of delegating. I feel it belongs under objectives because normally delegation has to do with situations that are not covered in a formal job description. Here we take objectives as referring not only to corporate and departmental, but also to individual responsibilities.

The Need for Job Descriptions

The extent to which you grasp this need may determine largely the relevance of this book to your future. I hope you will see how this subject can relate to your own situation. It is my absolute conviction that all of us in Christian work should have job descriptions and those job descriptions should be living, dynamic tools like the organizational structure. A job description, if not reviewed with the people concerned, the boss and the subordinate, at least once a year, up-dated, retyped, and re-issued, is antiquated. It may be doing more harm than good.

Job descriptions are very important. A job description helps us know what our tasks are and why we are in the organization. A job description helps our boss to know what we are doing. It helps us to know what he expects of us, and it lets people around us know what we are doing. Likewise we know why their jobs exist. Very few people in industry have job descriptions. Many businesses do not have job descriptions. If they do, often they are unrelated, irrelevant, out of date, and quite a caricature—not really representative of what the person is doing.

The more technical and specific and routine the function, the easier it is to write the job description, but the less the description is needed. The more innovative, creative, and imaginative the job, the greater the need for the job description, but the more difficult to write. For example, a person doing linguistic work is assigned to a tribe to reduce a language to writing. It is easy, relatively speaking, to write that person's job description. But a job assigned to a church planter is very difficult to write, yet this person needs a description even more than the linguist.

Take a situation in the Missionary Aviation Fellowship (MAF). It will be a great deal easier to write the job description of a person whose job is to repair engines than it is to write the job description for the person who is the Field Director. The more managerial the job, the more difficult to write the description. But the more managerial the function, the more important it is to write the job description.

Even if you are in a voluntary situation where you are not paid, job descriptions are still important. Some of the most effective churches I know in America have job descriptions for their deacons and their Sunday school superintendents and their Sunday school teachers. And you might think that people stand off and say, "Oh, I don't want a job description. I'm just serving the Lord." But these people say, "I'm glad to know what is expected of me." It puts teeth into our organizational structure, and it gives clarity to relationships. More than any other single device, job descriptions give us a goal-orientation.

The best job descriptions are specific, definite, and measurable. They have teeth; they are binding; they are clear.

Sometime ago I gave a seminar lecture on job descriptions and then assigned the people to write down their own job descriptions. Here is one job description I received. It followed my suggested format: the job summary, the job duties, the organizational relationships, the qualifications, and the development.

Job Description

To live in a certain village in such a spiritual, Christ-honoring way as to turn residents of this village from darkness to light.

Duties	1. To maintain a constant fellowship with God, so as to live a sinless, perfect example in dependence on the Holy Spirit.
	2. Be ready at all times to give a reason for the hope that is in you.
	3. Give unselfishly of time and talents to any worthy cause within the village which might result in winning some villagers to Christ.
	4. Write a report at least once a month.
Organizational Relationships	1. Responsible to God alone, he will judge the quick and the dead.
	2. Responsible for those in the village whom God has predestinated to enter into his glorious fellowship.
Qualifications	Should be a spiritually-minded person of highest integrity. If possible, should have completed Bible School.
Training and Development	Should be skilled in using the Word of God for the winning of precious souls.

In the light of what I said the job description ought to be, this job description is ambiguous and has no measurement, but it sounds so spiritual! Do you know what good this will do? It will just inflate the man's already over-inflated spiritual ego.

The job description format you use is unimportant. Go to the library and check a hundred books on management in which the subject of job descriptions is dealt with and you will find a hundred suggestions or formats. For example, there was an article recently on how to write a job description for a pastor. The format was altogether different than what I would suggest, but in the end it accomplished the same thing. Generally, job descriptions come out at the same place, though the building of them is entirely different.

Writing the Job Description

At the beginning of your job description you need a job title. The job title should be as descriptive as possible of the work that is performed. Where you are involved with precedent and tradition and cannot make changes, use whatever terms the situation dictates. The title should describe as nearly as possible the work that is being filled or accomplished by this position. Then, you need the name of the individual involved. There are only two places where the specific individual is brought into play—at the top of the sheet and in the last point, training and development.

The other sections of this job description could apply to any individual. Next, write the date. This is important because after twelve months have elapsed, the job description is out of date! There are very few job descriptions that can go on for more than a year without alterations, because the environment changes, the capacities of the individual change, and the needs of the office change. The person managing has to keep this constantly in review. In more intricate, complex situations you may want to indicate the department or the division. For example, a person may be in the evangelism department, the church-planting department, or the radio department of a mission, or may be in the laboratory department of a hospital. This simply further breaks down and pinpoints where this person fits in the organization.

The job description consists of five parts:

1. *The job summary.* The most difficult section to write, the job summary reflects the position on the organizational chart. The job summary is built into that total pyramid (see page 68). There should be a short-range and a long-range pyramid. The job summary places a person into the pyramid where he or she belongs, and is aimed at accomplishing the goal of the total organization. The job summary puts in words the end result this position exists to accomplish. When you ask people for whom you are responsible to begin working on their own job descriptions, you may find that they do not know why they are there. This has to do with purpose, with objectives, with goals, with targets. You may discover that you have positions that exist without valid reason. If you take this matter seriously, you will find that there are people on the payroll involved in the activities that have no definitive, specific purpose. The job summary must be measurable, definitive and specific.

2. *The job duties.* These are the activities necessary for the accomplishment of the above-mentioned end result. This is the easiest to write, particularly if persons just write down what they presently are doing. But that is not writing a job description. You have merely given a person a piece of paper to justify the continuation of his or her activities, and that may be bad. Do not tackle *duties* until you have settled the end result.

   Once the end result is identified, list the activities that are necessary for the accomplishment of it. Here you begin to draw some very distinct lines between the various positions that exist in your organization, and begin to eliminate overlap. This can help the function of an organization where a leader, while retaining an extremely sensitive team-consciousness and concept, recognizes "I'm praying for this person over here who is doing so and so, but that is his job and this is mine." The leader is concerned and is involved, available to help if needed. But that particular task belongs to someone else and the leader does not interfere. The manager is not going to make another person's decision. The manager has his or her own work to do.

3. *Organizational relationships.* Here we are back to the organizational chart. Organizational relationships extend in four directions: up, down, and sideways in both directions. This should show a subordinate the exact relationship to a superior, the exact relationship to his or her subordinate, and the exact relationship to the people on either side. This works in a church where a Sunday school department leader realizes "I take my orders with respect to the operation of this Sunday school from So and So. I am responsible to oversee these people. I know there is another department functioning over here and this person has the same kind of authority and responsibility that I have." You do not have to pay a person a salary to do this. It works beautifully in a voluntary situation like a Sunday school or in a more complex situation like General Motors. The two key words are *to* and *for*. *Responsible to* shows superiors; *responsible for* designates subordinates.

It is important to note the difference between *staff* and *line* relationships. A staff relationship means service, information, consultation, and advice. This person or committee has no authority, does not issue any orders. In the chart, the broken line indicates a staff relationship overagainst a line relationship. In other words, this person or group serves in an advisory capacity rather than in an authoritative and decision-making role.

4. *Qualifications.* This is what the person should ideally be and know in order to most effectively

accomplish the job summary. If you omit the individual's name then you can write job descriptions for functions you eventually want accomplished in your organization, for which you neither have personnel nor money now. This helps tremendously. It is not a matter of who is available; it is a matter of "here is what we want done. Where is the person that can best do it?" That makes a difference in filling positions in your church. Here is what we are trying to accomplish and what needs to be done in this position. Here are the qualifications. Where is the individual? Set your standard high, but keep it realistic.

At this point specify the job description under the heading of Training and Development.

5. *Training and development.* A person does not ever measure up fully to the qualifications the job requires. He or she needs self-development to better qualify. We are speaking here about skills and abilities, about learning to do better the job we have been called by God to do. That is self-development. If the key to training and development is that it must be specific, then training and development must project itself for no more than twelve months.

This person does not quite measure up. No one does. If someone does, revise your qualifications and get that person up higher. What training and development can we give to this individual to better qualify him or her? You do not unilaterally determine this and hand it to that person on a slip of paper as you go past one morning. This is a mutually agreed thing. Individuals will be harder on themselves than you would be if you let them be. Do not think of training and development as just going to school. Learning does occur without going to a university. There are other places to develop your skills. For example, one of our men needed development in a certain area. We did some research and found, as far as we were able to determine, the one man in America that knew more about this subject than any other man. We wrote to him and said, "If we send our man out, can he sit at your elbow for a couple of weeks and just watch what you do?" That is training and development.

Training and development says, "Mr. A. is going to California. He is going to be an understudy with Mr. B. from October 1 to October 15. It will cost us 'X' number of dollars." That is training and development. It may include formal situations. Training and development does not necessarily mean going back to a formal study situation. That is not the kind of training and development most of us need. Sometimes we may need a Dale Carnegie course, or a rapid-reading course, or a course in public relations, or a course in some skill that relates to the type of work that we are doing. This training and development is specific. It is dated. It is to compensate for the person's inadequacies as they are spelled out in this list of qualifications. I know this is work, but it will transform any operation you are in—if you will do it.

9 Encourage the Troops

Management-Leading Principles

There is a vast difference between problem identification and problem solving. Problem solving, comparatively speaking is easy. Problem identification is extremely difficult.

Under the subject of management leading comes decision making and communicating. Leading is the work in which we engage to inspire and, where necessary, impel people to take action. But to lead effectively, we must know how to make decisions and how to communicate effectively.

Decision making

A manager has been described as a person who makes decisions; sometimes right ones, sometimes wrong ones, but a manager always makes them. We must not insist on infallibility in decision making for people who work with us, nor in ourselves.

If you are in a place of leadership you have to make decisions. Hesitancy in deciding will breed demoralization and frustration among your subordinates. The longer it takes a person to get a decision from you, the more encumbered he or she is, and the more you are saying, "Your time and activities are of minimal importance."

Why do we have such difficulties in making decisions? One major reason is the control-orientation of our organization. We would prefer to have everyone involved in the decision than to have the decision made quickly, effectively and thereby accomplish our goal. To make decisions involves risk. Many people hedge on decision making and would prefer to do anything rather than to decide.

Decision-Making Principles

Three principles apply to decision making.

1. *A logical decision can be reached only if the problem is first defined.* There is a vast difference between problem identification and problem solving. Problem solving, comparatively speaking, is easy. Problem identification is extremely difficult. Most of us do not take time to identify problems. We plunge in to solve them. Problems, because they are related to human beings, are often covered with a facade—one of the chief characteristics of the human being. When you sit down with a man and say, "How are you?" he will seldom tell you right off how he really is. Suppose a person comes to you for counseling. "Tell me what your problem is," you begin.

The individual will seldom immediately describe the real problem. Because problems are so intimately entwined with human emotions, we have difficulty facing the heart of the problem. We must be careful to avoid dealing with just the symptoms, while ignoring the real problem. We must persevere to adequately define the problem.

2. *The principle of adequate evidence teaches us that a logical decision must be valid in terms of the evidence on which it is based.* Our problem in God's work is our utter subjectivity which builds a high protective wall around us so that everything about us is immune to the criticism of our colleagues because we have prayed about it, or the Lord has led us. I am not speaking lightly of prayer or divine guidance. But if we are not very careful, this subjectivity can become a protective wall around us to keep us from the truth.

3. *The principle of identity or scope teaches us that facts may appear to differ, depending on the point of view and the point in time from which they are observed.* In other words, the decisions we make are valid or invalid depending on how and when we look at them. This is why some decisions made today look so stupid tomorrow.

The Logical Thinking Process

The logical thinking process consists of a series of questions. I do not expect that you are going to take these questions and apply them to every decision. But if you can apply them to major decisions, they will help you immeasurably. They will form a pattern in your subconscious mind that can be adapted to various types of problem situations.

1. *What is the apparent problem?* What do you think is the problem? It may not be the real problem.

2. *What are the facts?* Because some of us are exclusively theologically oriented and think we have a

pipeline to omniscience, we cannot afford to be bothered with the assimilation of facts. After all, we have revelation! Somebody once asked, "Are you gathering facts or merely rearranging your prejudices?" You need to get the situation factor, the people factor, the place factor, the time factor, the causative factor, and then assimilate all the facts you can.

3. *What is the real problem?* Do not ask this question until you have adequately dealt with the two previous ones. Remember the facade!

4. *What are the possible solutions?* Generally, the possible solutions that emerge spontaneously to mind will be extremes. That is the way we solve problems instinctively. We just get hold of the pendulum and swing as hard as we can from one extreme to the other. These extreme solutions may need to be considered, but do not settle for two alternative and diametrically opposed solutions. *There is always a third solution.* It will seldom manifest itself easily, but do not stop until you find a third solution to the problem. When you find the third, you will often find that it will open up a whole new vista with a fourth, fifth, and sixth possible solution.

5. *Which course of action shall we follow?* This involves implementation of the course chosen. Risk becomes a prime factor. If you have a "safety first" mentality, all of your analysis and fact assimilation will come to nothing here.

These questions outline the total analysis required by any decision, large or small: Do I really understand the problem? What am I trying to get done? Is this the way to do it? What will go wrong when I put this decision into action?

You are not going to solve one problem without creating others. However, you hope to create lesser problems. Nevertheless, in most problem solving there are some negative consequences. Anticipate them. What is going to go wrong when I put this decision into effect?

Communication

What is communication? Here is a definition from the Word of God. In this passage there is one word which, more than any other word, tells us what communication is.

> And even things without life giving sound, whether pipe or harp, except they give a distinction in the sounds, how shall it be known what is piped or harped? For if the trumpet give an uncertain sound, who shall prepare himself to the battle? So, likewise ye, except ye utter by the tongue words easy to be understood, how shall it be known what is spoken? For ye shall speak into the air. (1 Cor. 14:7–9, KJV).

It is the word *understood* that is so important. Communication is the work we do to secure understanding between ourselves and another human being.

David Sarnoff of RCA said, "The power to communicate is the power to lead." I do not think anyone who has been involved in a managerial position will doubt this assertion.

Principles of Communication

In management leading there are three principles which apply to communication:

1. Line loss. The effectiveness of communication tends to vary inversely with its extension. Suppose I took fifteen people, lined them up around the room, and then read in the ear of one person a headline from the morning paper. By the time that headline was transmitted orally from person to person around the room, there would be little or no resemblance with what came from person fifteen as compared with

what went into person one! The effectiveness of communication tends to vary inversely with its extension. The more levels it has to go through, the more minds and tongues that filter it, the more distorted it becomes. There is no sense in getting angry about this and there is no sense in blaming people when something is repeated back to you, fifth- or sixth-hand, and you are quoted incorrectly.

2. *Emotional appeal.* Appeals to emotions are communicated more readily than appeals to reason. If preachers could get hold of this it could revolutionize their preaching. We are so logical. We follow such strict forms of apologetics and we have everything unanswerably set forth. The only problem is that no one hears it. It does not grip anyone. Study the great teachers and preachers of history and you will find that they have always found emotional pegs on which to hang their thoughts.

3. *Application.* The more specific communication is used and applied, the better it will be understood and remembered. Some of us do a lot of talking but not much teaching—a lot of preaching but not much communicating. Why? Because maybe we say it only once or twice, or a dozen times, and that is not enough. Sometimes a thing has to be said over and over and over again.

The big problem in communication is words, because words tend to obscure and not clarify meaning. According to the Oxford English Dictionary, the five hundred most-used words in the English language have an average of twenty-three meanings each. The word *round* has seventy distinctly different meanings. This is not the only problem we face.

The problem that we are confronted with is that we have a man with an idea. He wants to communicate that idea to another person. How is he going to transmit an idea from his brain to the other person's brain? It can be a theological, mechanical, or philosophical idea. Obviously, his first recourse is going to be words. They may be written or spoken, softly or loudly. Words are the main instrument at his disposal to communicate or transmit this idea from his mind to another human being's mind. The words may have one meaning in the mind of the speaker, but a completely different meaning in the mind of the hearer.

Dr. Howard Hendricks of Dallas Theological Seminary describes the difficulty in conveying not just a concept but a "concept feeling." His point is that we do not convey only concepts. That is impossible. We convey "concept feelings." The two are inseparable. It is not just a cold idea. It is an idea that is coupled with feeling. Sometimes it is an intense feeling; sometimes not so intense; sometimes a negative feeling; sometimes a feeling of hate or love. Still there is a feeling to some degree connected with every concept, and these feelings color our hearing.

Four Stages of Communication

Why do we get into such trouble when it comes to communication? Because there are four stages in the process of communication and often we go astray at each stage.

WE BEGIN WITH THE ALL-IMPORTANT PROCESS OF ASK-ING. We do not adequately communicate with another until we have asked questions. I must know the person's mind to some degree before I can communicate with him. The complexity and the intricacies of the message determine how much I must know about that person's mind. For example, if I want to say, "Shut the door," I do not have to know a great deal about the person or his or her thinking processes to communicate that concept. But let us say I want to communicate a theological or philosophical idea to this person. A thousand things can enter in here—birthplace, upbringing, family situation, education, books read in the last five years.

How do I discover what another human being is like? By looking at skin color? By looking at eye color? By looking at weight? No! These are externals. They have nothing to do with what is inside the person. There is one way you get to the person on the inside and that is to ask questions. Some of us do not communicate simply because we either do not have the time to ask questions or we do not know how to ask questions.

There are three basic types of questions:

The informational type question has to do with statistics and facts. Questions like: How many? Who? How much? Where? When? Informational questions are inoffensive questions. You can always say to a person, "Where do you work?" "How many people are involved?" without getting a negative reaction.

The ideational type question asks people what they think or what they suggest or what they feel. Like informational questions, ideational questions are also safe. You will not create trouble or give offense when you are asking a subordinate an ideational question.

The evaluation type question is always dangerous. This type asks people to evaluate their work, ideas, concepts, or anything with which they are associated or involved. These kinds of questions are strategic and tend to become tremendously subjective. If you ask evaluative questions of an individual before you have asked ideational or informational questions you may alienate that person. We are what we are and it is a proven fact that we are more willing to give evaluative information after we have had an opportunity to express our ideas and to give information, particularly information which we feel the other person may not have about us or our work. We need to ask questions that fit the need.

In all of this I am suggesting that you ask "open questions" not "closed questions." Open questions invite the
other people to express freely what they feel. They never
make a person feel boxed in. This is an open question:
"Tell me, Joe, how does this problem look to you?" Joe
can go on from that to express what he really feels. A
closed question is a kind of question that forces the other
person to a point of view other than his or her own. It is a
kind of question that makes people feel like they have to
conform to what we already think. Here is a closed question: "Now, Joe, if you were convinced that taking this
action is morally wrong, you wouldn't be for it would
you?" What can Joe say? You have closed him out.

Ask leading questions, not loaded ones! Leading questions give direction to the reply but they are not restric-
tive to any one way. Here is a leading question: "How did
you go about working out your solution to the problem,
Joe?" A loaded question puts the respondent in a difficult
position—whatever the answer may be. An example of a
loaded question is: "What made you think that your
solution to the problem was the right one?" You have
made the person defensive. Defensiveness is one of the
most detrimental and continuously recurring attitudes in
Christian work. Not hatred. Not animosity. Not bitter-
ness. I see these things occasionally, but the most univer-
sal attitude I find in Christian work is defensiveness.

Ask cool questions and not heated ones. The cool question appeals to reason and involves the emotion as little
as possible. A heated question, on the other hand, reflects
the feeling of the questioner and incites the feelings of the
respondent. Here is a cool question: "Now what would
you say the first step toward a solution should be, Joe?"
And the heated question: "We've already been round and
round on that one, so what do you think we should do?"
The person has to produce then and there or be embar-
rassed.

THE SECOND STEP IN THE COMMUNICATION PROCESS IS
TELLING, ARTICULATING, PUTTING IN WORDS THE MESSAGE

YOU HAVE TO GET ACROSS. Unfortunately, we often plunge into telling before we have done any asking. How do we go about telling? (I am going to digress considerably from purely managerial communication situations to talk about communications in general because most of you who read this book are preachers and teachers.) How do we communicate our message from our minds to the minds of a group of people? Here are four steps to good telling.

1. *Get an audience.* Attract attention! Here is a brain that is in absolute neutral, an emotion that is disengaged, an anatomy in which no capacity for receiving communication is presently functioning. The person may be in church or in Sunday school or in a seminar, but there he or she sits—in neutral! Getting an audience is not easy.

   There was a farmer who sold a mule to a person down the road. He explained carefully to the purchaser, "This mule is a good ole mule but you must be gentle with him, ever so gentle."

   The next day about ten o'clock, the purchaser appeared at the door of the seller, most irate, demanding his money back. The seller said, "What's wrong?"

   "That mule is sitting in the middle of the barnyard and will not move. I have been ever so gentle all morning with him and there he sits."

   "Oh," the seller said, "Let me help you."

   So they went down to the purchaser's barnyard and there sat the mule. The farmer looked around the barnyard. He got a big stick and walked over to the mule and hit him as hard as he could right on the head. The old mule staggered around and got up on his feet. The purchaser said,

   "But I thought you said you had to be gentle."

   "You do, but first you have to get his attention!"

   We often talk without getting anyone's attention.

2. *Build a bridge.* Build a bridge from what you say to what a person is interested in. I like young people. I would rather smell perfume than liniment! I like young people—their imagination, their drive, their color, the sparkle in their eyes. Frankly, I do not think that all young people have deteriorated. But, the one complaint I hear most frequently from young people about preaching in America is, "Well, what's all that got to do with where I am? Why bring that up? We hear these learned dissertations on this and that subject, but they are wide of the mark. They make no point of contact with us." We cannot get through to people until we learn to build a bridge from where we are to where they are.

3. *Illustrate!* You may have heard Dr. Donald Grey Barnhouse preach. In my estimation, Dr. Barnhouse was one of the greatest illustrators ever and also one of the best communicators. I would recommend that you read his sermons and books. The man was masterful. Also study the illustrations of the New Testament. You will find in most instances Bible illustrations use things that people handle and with which they are thoroughly conversant and familiar.

4. *Ask for action.* We might say this about almost any communication. There is a sense in which the whole point of a communication is to ask for action.

Sue Nichols, in *Words on Target* says that there are three essential ingredients in communication.

Communicate *economically.* There must be economy in our communication. Economy in communication means communicating without any unnecessary words. If you are a preacher or teacher, play back one of your sermons or lectures sometime. Listen to the superfluous words. What do they do? They obstruct communication.

Communicate with words of energy, words of force. How long has it been since you added a new word to your vocabulary? This is one easy thing you can do. You probably have access to the *Reader's Digest*. Work those little vocabulary builders. Make it a point to learn at least one new word every week and make sure it is an easy word. Make sure the word carries an impact.

You may have heard Dr. R. G. Lee, one of the greatest preachers of our day, an orator par excellence. Somebody was complimenting Lee one day on a sermon.

They said, "Dr. Lee, the thing that is so unforgettable is your choice of words."

He said, "Oh, don't talk to me about words. I struggle with words."

We do not take our vocabulary very seriously. Work on it. Discover words of energy.

Communicate by *subtlety*. Ms. Nichols's point is that we must be the readers' eyes and ears, but we dare not be their brain or will.

LISTENING IS THE THIRD STAGE IN THE PROCESS OF COMMU-NICATION. We have tried to learn how to do almost everything except listen. Andrew Carnegie said, "Any fool can speak with a glib tongue. Send me a man who listens." A lot of us do not communicate because we do not listen. How many times people have said about another person, "I cannot get his ear." This is a sad commentary. Learn how to listen.

THE FINAL STAGE IN THE PROCESS OF COMMUNICATION IS UNDERSTANDING. This means that two human beings understand each other. Notice that communication is not agreement, it is understanding. There is a lot more misunderstanding than there is disagreement among God's people. It is a strategic fact that the greater the level of understanding between people, the higher the level of tolerance of disagreement.

Formal vs. Informal Communication

Let me clarify the difference between formal and informal communication. By formal communication we mean those words or letters by which we endeavor to formulate or convey a concept from ourselves to another person.

But this is not the only way we communicate. We communicate not only by what we say but also by how we say it, by our posture, our facial expressions, by the way we dress. Everything about us communicates! When a person drums his fingers on the table or desk, what does this say? It says volumes. "I'm bored and you are not important, so hurry up." It makes a difference how we carry ourselves, whether our shoulders are back or slumped. Do we not communicate by a positive attitude as overagainst a negative attitude? Do we not communicate by a spring in our step rather than a slouch in our walk? Everything about us communicates. This is why we need to consider everything that we are in our communication: the way we dress, the way we live, the way we express ourselves. This is informal communication.

What are the barriers to communication? Where do we get into trouble? What causes our problems? Undoubtedly the biggest problem is our mistaking the medium for the process. Let me illustrate. I was conducting some meetings in a church in Michigan. After one of the meetings, a group of us were standing around in the basement of the church having coffee. The pastor's wife entered the room and she was what one might call a "female dreadnaught." She steamed up to where I was, her eyes flaming with indignation. I stood there wondering whether to speak or run. After some minutes, I said, "Hello," but she just puffed and steamed. Finally I said, "Is something wrong?" Well, that pushed her button.

She said, "Those crazy women!"

I said, "Which women?"

She replied, "Those dumb women in our church."

I said, "Tell me about them."

Well, did she ever tell me! Her whole point was "I told these people! I TOLD THESE WOMEN!" And I could not say it to her, but I thought to myself, "Yes, she told them, but that is not important. The important thing is, *did they hear her?*" It is an amazing thing. I can stand, or you can stand, in the presence of other people and tell and tell and tell and still have them say, "Nobody ever told me." It happens every day of the week to everyone of us.

My seventeen-year-old son came out one day with something that he had discovered. I had been telling him the same thing for seventeen years. He never heard it, but he heard someone else say it and it registered. What was my reaction? "Well, that's great! A great discovery, Dave! I am happy for you. Terrific!" I'm not going to tell him, "Why, I told you that!" What difference does it make? We have an exaggerated concept of the significance of what we have to say. The other person does not care what we have to say. When you mistake the medium for the process you have not communicated. You may have told until you were hoarse. Communication is not telling. Communication is asking., telling, listening, and then creating understanding. It is nothing less than that. Communication is not writing a memo, for that does not insure understanding.

The other barrier to communication is the failure to consider emotional blocks. The fact, whether we like it or not, is that we are dealing with emotional creatures. You have something to tell someone who may be inwardly distraught about things that he or she cannot divulge to you or anyone else. That person is not going to hear what you say because of preoccupation with a personal distraction. Perhaps the person is ill, not in enough pain to warrant going to bed, but when a person is in pain there is preoccupation with that pain and the person does not hear everything that goes on around. Maybe the person is distressed about a child. Or maybe something, in all innocence, was said two hours earlier which hurt that person. You may preach that self and feelings should not be felt. There is an element of truth in this, but we must remember that we are human beings.

We are communicating with people who are human beings. The Lord Jesus understood people, their feelings, their needs and he was sympathetic. He knew how to say precisely the right word to an adulteress. He knew exactly how to deal tenderly with those obstinate, impenetrable minds of the disciples. Read, *The Training of the Twelve*, by A. B. Bruce. See the marvelous empathy the Lord Jesus had for those men in their obstinacy, in their darkness— the amazing ability of projecting his personality into the disciples and so fully understanding them. The Lord had this empathy for all whom he met. When he raised Jairus' daughter from the dead, the first thing he said was, "Give her something to eat." We would have been more interested in getting a tract written, but not the Lord Jesus. "Give her something to eat."

10 Evaluate the Results

Management-Controlling Principles and Styles

Remember that the followers of the Lord Jesus Christ are called sheep *and the continuing need of any sheep is a shepherd. We recognize this spiritually and we appoint undershepherds but this is equally important in the practical outworkings of our lives.*

Management-Controlling Principles

One definition of management controlling is, "the work we engage in to check work in progress and complete it." This is one area of Christian work that perplexes me greatly. How have we come to assume that we can be

119

thrown in together as a group of individuals with the view of accomplishing common goals without someone assuming the responsibility for checking and coordinating the work in progress? But often no one does. In our types of organization we come up with a whole series of people, it can be fifty or 125, allegedly banded together and moving toward an objective like the evangelization of a community and the planting of the church in that area. Yet, in the final outworking instead of moving in union and harmony, the tendency is for each individual to follow the path of his or her own inclination. Dedicated persons go in all kinds of directions with goals that may be similar but are seldom coordinated.

The point of management controlling is, once the goal has been identified, once the relationships have been determined, once the work has been assigned, once the decision-making power or authority has been clearly defined, to insure that we all go in one direction and work in harmony. No one is more aware of the problems of control than I am and yet I still presume to emphasize that the problem can be overcome. Do not assume that your organization is so different, that everyone is just simply too individualistic. We can expect to achieve this kind of union toward our objective. It can be done.

Management control must be implemented to accomplish our common goal. How shall we describe missions and churches, generally? We have a manager at the top, frequently insecure and very unsure of what a manager is supposed to do. Often the person is so totally oblivious of the value of management controlling, that he or she simply assumes or hopes that everyone will move toward the objective when a little pressure is exerted and the work is committed to God in prayer. Frequently, when objectives are not being accomplished, but while there is work being done and signs of activity are evident, those in positions of leadership do not take any action. But, as the situation deteriorates and worsens, leaders begin to be concerned.

They begin to pray. They should go further and implement management control. An individual responsible for
the group should begin to check the work in progress
against the established performance standards.

I think we harm our Christian workers when we defer
to their demands to be individualists and let them wander
all over the place without reining them in tight, controlling their activities and saying, "Here is the direction we
are going. We are trying to accomplish this. Here is your
role. Now play that role." We all have come into the
Lord's work because of the strong goal orientation. Indi-
vidualism emerges after we are in the group, not before. It
is not the result of what we were before we got into the
group. We came into the group because we wanted to
move in union with other persons toward the accomplishment of the goal. What is the problem? The problem is
leadership. There usually is not a goal-oriented leader at
the top who gives the order and says, "We are going to do
this. Here is your role." Eventually the leader may have to
go back and say, "Excuse me, Joe, we blundered on the
project. I am awfully sorry. Now let us try again and
go toward this goal." But this seldom happens. Some of
you may come from highly goal-oriented missions where
there is adequate management pressure at the top to
move people in unison, but generally speaking this is
not so.

We must always respect people as human beings, not
pieces of machinery, not just inanimate objects that you
place in a certain spot and say, "Do this," and they do it.
No, these are human beings, but they are human beings
who want to accomplish a goal.

Occasionally you will meet a Christian worker who
does not want to accomplish anything. Sometimes you
will have to remove that person from the pursuit of this
goal and send him or her home. If a man embezzled
$60,000, you would remove him. If a man became in-
volved in heresy, you would ship him off. But people can

wander around ineffectively on the field, and we do not do anything about it. I want to insist that it is not their fault. It is the leader's fault; or maybe we should say, it is the people at the top.

So many things begin to merge here and come to the fore: the goal orientation, organization, the job description, communications, establishing and maintaining human inter-relationships, the authority by which we manage. However, the persons who are wandering aimlessly around are not to blame. Let us remember that the followers of the Lord Jesus Christ are called *sheep* and the continuing need of any sheep is a shepherd. We recognize this spiritually and we appoint undershepherds, but this is equally important in the practical outworkings of our lives.

Management controlling is concerned with ineffective and vague leadership. Admittedly, the longer the organization has been in existence, the more difficulties we are going to have. Leadership can change! But with great effort. Still we can change, provided we are willing to pay the price and the leaders are sufficiently goal oriented and courageous.

The Establishment
of Performance Standards

Do you know when management control begins with a missionary, or with a person taking over a Sunday school department in the church, or with the individual who is taking the job in the office of the Bible Society, or with the one who is coming into a strategic position in the hospital? Performance standards must be started *before* the person starts to work. Missionary societies need to do this with their candidates before they ever sign on the dotted line and the home board accepts them. Do you know what kind of people you will attract when you clearly state the objectives of the group and the responsibilities of each individual? You will attract the courageous, the goal-oriented, the self-effacing, the self-sacrificing. Always! But the standards have to be determined ahead of time. If they are not, and you have to go back and pick up the pieces, then it is more difficult. Even in an old organization where people go and come when they desire, it can be done. One day a lady who has visited a number of mission fields, said to me, "Do you know the great tragedy on the mission field? The great tragedy is there is not *must!* No 'I *must* get up!' 'I *must* have my devotions.' 'I *must* study.' 'I *must* finish this language exam.' 'I *must* see these people.' 'I *must* prepare for this conference.'" Management controlling forces us to put the *must* back into our work.

Management controlling is concerned with having an agreement with the individual that these are the standards toward which we are aiming. These standards are not unilaterally determined and handed down to the individual. Mr. A, up at the top, does not come along to a worker and say, "Look, you are going to do such and such." How does he do it? Mr. A, either on the field or back in the homeland, comes along and says, "Now listen, our goal is this. Here are your gifts. Here is your calling according to your testimony. What standards of performance do you feel we should aim at together to accomplish this?" People will always be more exacting with themselves than you would be with them, if you were to devise the standard unilaterally.

Then put the standard of performance in writing. It is amazing how illiterate we become when it comes to management! We will not write things. My first question to people with managerial problems is, "Does this fellow know his problem?" My second question is, "Is it written down and does he have a copy and do you have a copy?" The answer ninety-nine times out of a hundred is "No." *We must write down the standard of performance and give the person involved a copy.*

We who are in positions of leadership are required to love those under us supremely, but at the same time to hold them to the highest standards. The person at the top must constantly watch the performance of subordinates. How many people should a leader manage? Only as many people as he or she can effectively manage. What happens when a leader cannot manage all of the people? Someone else should manage some of them. The people we usually elect to managerial positions are already so busy that they cannot possibly oversee and scrutinize the activities and procedures of others. But this is what is so absolutely essential.

Performance Measuring

The second demand of leadership is *performance measuring*. The person at the top must have some yardstick for measuring activities. What kind of measurements do we need? We need to know when a person gets up and when he or she goes to bed. We need to know how many vacation days are taken. We need to know when a furlough begins and ends. I have been in missions all of these years and I still do not understand how a missionary is permitted to just unilaterally determine, "I'm going home and I'm coming back. I'll let you know when." What kind of control is that?

Performance measuring is based on what we are doing and the goal we are collectively seeking to achieve. There are two elements: the standard of performance toward which we are aiming, and the person whose performance is being measured.

Psychology tells us that one of the basic drives of the human being is a desire to achieve. There is a fire burning in the breast of every individual to achieve something before he or she dies. This is especially true of everyone in your mission or they would not be missionaries. They would be back home earning money, storing it away, and living comfortably. When individuals seem to fight against management, they are not fighting because they are afraid that the superintendent or director is going to help them achieve something. They are fighting because they are afraid the director is going *to keep them from* achieving something. Such people are so individualistic that they do not want the missionary society to hinder them from accomplishing something for the Lord and his Kingdom. Management is not there to obstruct. While we push decisions down the ladder, what else do we send down? Concern, help, direction. The leader should be able to say, "Look, the whole purpose of our being banded together, having superiors and subordinates and job descriptions and organizational charts and decisions made, is to facilitate the accomplishment of the thing that God has given you to do."

Performance Evaluating

The third demand of leadership is *performance evaluating*, a little different from performance measuring. In my thinking, in performance measuring we are concerned about *one* person. In performance evaluating we are concerned about appraising the relative value of this person's activities in relation to the activities of co-workers. This becomes even more difficult than performance measuring because with performance measuring we are usually concerned with one individual; but with performance evaluating we are concerned with many individuals and their activities.

Performance Correcting

Finally, in the *performance correcting* aspect of leadership, we are concerned with coaching, with providing the "how" to people and, where necessary, correcting a situation that may have gone awry, always with the objective in view. Managers must not correct simply to satisfy their own desires or wishes. That is why goal orientation is a necessity.

Organizational Chart

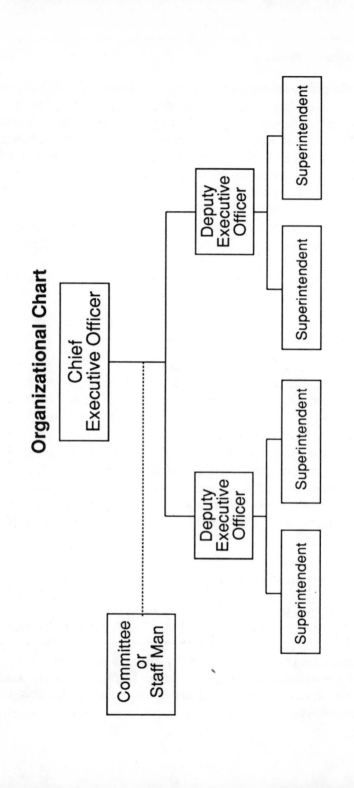

Management Styles

There are several styles of management. The *scientific management style* has maximum concern for accomplishment but people are merely tools for the accomplishment. This management style is a laborious or toilsome type of management; people are nothing more than necessary instruments or machines to accomplish tasks. This sort of management style often develops in religious situations. Generally, though not always, it is the product of the strong natural leader. It may be the product of a highly insecure but domineering leader. Scientific management has maximum concern for accomplishment but a regard for people that is subhuman.

The other extreme is *country club management* which says that the thing we are concerned about most is the happiness of these people. Whether or not we do anything is quite irrelevant. This is where people work together around a swimming pool with tall cold drinks at their elbows. Everybody is just happy, and at any gathering, or any situation, the whole concern is for happiness. This was epitomized in President Lyndon Johnson's speech one time when he turned to a heckler and said, "Why don't you people be happy?"—as though happiness is primo!

Another style, unfortunately, is *impoverished management.* This occurs when a person is neither motivated by a very great respect for the dignity of human personalities under his or her care, nor is the manager very much concerned about getting the product out the back door and on the truck and shipped. Do not make the mistake of assuming that this kind of management style does not exist in Christian circles. It does. Often enough many pastors fit this category. They are satisfied to maintain things as they are, concerned only that their job is secure.

Another style of management is a *compromise management.* It is neither dynamic not is it dormant. It is active, it is alive, but barely. It is a middle-of-the-road kind of management. Compromise managers want you to be happy, but not too happy. We will do anything to make you happy if it does not mean too much trouble. Certainly we want to achieve something. We really want to evangelize this country, but we are not going to sweat or toil about it. We are not going to get excited or "hot under the collar" about it. In a UCLA survey, it was discovered from the estimate of thousands of managers in top-middle-lower echelons in America that 65 percent of industrial managers adjust their management style to this position. What does that mean in regard to Christian managers? What percentage of people involved in religious work use compromise management?

There are other alternatives, but one style that often emerges is wide-arc *pendulum-swing management* where a person swings back and forth from one style of management to the other. An inspirational sermon shakes complacency, and the person makes sudden changes and clamps down on everybody. The result is that everybody becomes tense. Then someone comes along and says to the manager, "If you aren't good, we will not reelect you." So, swinging back over to a country-club position, the manager apologizes and seeks to smooth out the situation. That is the wide-arc pendulum-swing. Its chief characteristics are vacillation and inconsistency.

There is another position, the best one. *Concern management* is a combination of concern for people in its maximum manifestation with a concern for production or accomplishment to its absolute maximum. The Lord Jesus Christ epitomized this management style. He demonstrated the perfect combination of concern for people with concern for accomplishment.

Creativity, Commitment, and Conflict

There must be three basic issues in any wholesomely managed situation: creativity, commitment, and conflict. What do these various management styles do to the various issues?

Scientific Management

What does scientific management do to creativity? Remember this is a laborious, toilsome type of management. Every effort is made to accomplish and produce without showing any concern for the workers. In one sense, this is a very stimulating environment for creativity. However, it stimulates creativity in an anti-organizational way because it provokes people to figure out ways to beat the system.

Scientific management also creates high commitment, but again in anti-organizational ways. Usually people within the group form themselves around an insurrectionist who says, "Who cares for this society? Look how they are treating us! Let us join together and fight them."

Conflict is a necessary ingredient in human relationships. It was Lord Cromwell who said to one of his aides, "For heaven's sake, man, say 'no,' so I'll know there are two of us!" There must be wholesome conflict. But scientific management merely suppresses conflict. If a worker has a complaint, he is rebuked and told to keep quiet.

Country Club Management

What does country club management do with these elements? Country club management has a concern for happiness. As to creativity, it stifles it. There is no creativity in country club management because everyone wants things "as is" and is not willing to do any forward thinking. It creates very high commitment, but in narrow pro-organizational ways. This creates the centric group because it is oblivious to the goal. Country club management is never occupied with a worthwhile goal. Its goal is everyone's happiness. This management smothers conflict. Everything is fine. Please do not disturb.

Impoverished Management

In the impoverished management style, creativity does not exist. There is no creativity, imagination, or forward thinking. The only commitment that exists is the commitment of survival. Workers are committed insofar as it is necessary to keep donors from disappearing and to keep the mission from sending the manager home. As to conflict, it produces absolute neutrality. There is no differing of opinions. There is no peppering interaction that produces creativity and dynamics.

Compromise Management

The compromise management position characterizes most religious organizations. What does it do to creativity? Creativity is entirely directed toward personal survival. It does exist, not with respect to the work but with respect to personal survival. It is my work; these are my donors; this is my calling. Commitment, however, tends to be high, simply because in the compromise position a person has to be committed to survive. Workers are neither secure in what they are accomplishing, nor in their relationships with other people. So instead, they find security in a highly personalized description of tasks: "God led me to this place." So, what does this do to conflicts? Whenever there is conflict, there is splintering and compromise. There is neither substantial goal orientation to insure that the conflict is creative and wholesome, nor is there sufficient adjustment for keeping everyone happy. So this person gives a little, and somebody else gives a little, and the manager gives here and gives there.

Concern Management

In concern management creativity is high and stimulating; not only because a person knows that the manager recognizes value in dignity, but because the worker knows that the whole organization with which he or she is associated is out to accomplish the goal that the worker has personally espoused. Commitment is very high because individuals have a stake and a voice and are personally involved. Effective management does not reduce involvement but increases involvement in decision making. Regarding conflict, warm interaction and a sharp exchange of ideas often occur because issues are confronted head on. They are not suppressed. There must be a warm conflict, not personal hatred nor personal animosity, but personal interaction that is stimulating and dynamic. Otherwise, one person with a group of puppets or figures could do as much as a whole group is doing. Conflict surfaces when persons are pushed to be individuals on their own. Conflict does not necessarily mean fighting; perhaps the phrase *creative tension* would better describe it. Interaction, the idea of each person acting on the other, brings people up to their best. Generally people suppress interaction because the manager is afraid it is going to reflect on some of his or her deficiencies.

Conformity

Conformity of behavior is essential, but conformity in ideas is tragic. When we conform in our ideas, and everybody has to think the same things, we stagnate. Many missionary societies are in a state of stagnation today. From time to time the sharing of our ideas on various aspects of our work, such as finance and furloughs, produces a healthy situation. We need to encourage and stimulate our co-workers to express themselves. However, we do not implement everything that occurs to us. We must have a system of evaluation, scrutinizing, appraising, and testing before we implement. Sometime ago I talked to a candidate who had been turned down by a mission. I may be wrong, but my estimate of the situation was that they turned him down because he was too creative. I do not think he will go to the mission field now. That is too bad.

Picture a missionary organization of three hundred people represented by twenty-five charts. When new workers come in, usually they are placed in the lower echelon of the chart. They have a specific function and

assignment, and, incidentally, it should be made clear to
the new workers that even though they are low on the
chart they are not inferior socially. Each position is vital
to the function and goal of the organization; but unfortunately, most people think only of status.

A new worker is accepted by the missionary organization. In a lot of missions they say, "So you are joining our
group. For a year, or two years, you will not have any vote;
for a term you will be a junior missionary and will not
have any say. Please keep silent." Is this right? Or is there
a better way? Do we need a screening process where the
mentality and the goal and the function of the group is
adequately represented to these workers so that when
they come in they are a part of the organization? Why do
we stifle new personnel? Because we are afraid, we are
insecure, we are not sure where we stand and where we
are going, what we are doing, and how to do it. The
moment new people come into our mission, or into our
church, our mission and our church change. The addition
of one personality to our church alters that church. We
have to carefully screen so that we do not get people in
who are undesirable, but let us prayerfully determine
what is undesirable.

Epilogue: What Now?

Management offers tools that can help you if you use them. But the very best tools are useless unless you use them.

T he purpose of this book was to *introduce* the subject of management to Christian workers. Do not assume that you know everything about management because you have read this book. If this is all you have ever studied or read on the subject of management, then you know very little. To give anyone the impression (or to be under the impression yourself) that you are a knowledgeable person in the field of management will only lead to trouble. This book is an introduction to the subject. What you do after this is of real significance. Hundreds of people have come to my management seminars. However, only 10 to 15 percent of those who attend ever do anything about what they learn. Many people go away and talk about it; they have been impressed, and some are even excited about the relevance of much of this material. But that is not enough! A little knowledge is very dangerous, particularly when it comes to management. Successful management takes work. Work. You have to experiment. You have to revise it. You have to adapt it. You have to discuss it. It is worthwhile if you presevere.

Another point is to not assume that this is a substitute for something else. It is not a substitute for prayer, nor for the fullness of the Holy Spirit. Management offers tools that can help you if you use them. But the very best tools are useless unless you use them.

Do not start telling people how much you know. You will alienate them. They will resent your possessing knowledge that they do not have, and you might even get your neck in a good tight noose if you are not very careful. Do something before you do a lot of talking. Start with yourself, with your job description, your own objectives, your own organizational chart. Start with an effort to appraise your own communication. Start with yourself. You will share your knowledge best by example, not by word, and if you apply words too soon, you are going to be in real trouble.

Many management teachers have emphasized that if you are ever to do anything with management, you will begin it within two weeks after the basic exposure. Areas that you do not begin working on within two weeks, you will probably not do anything about. Three months from now you will go right back to the "tyranny of the urgent" at the expense of the important. It happens to hundreds of people, not just those in Christian work, but in industry too. Young executives go away to a seminar. They come back and their desks are piled high. Immediately they feel that they must deal with everything that is on their desks. These seem to be the urgent matters. Management is important, but the pressures of the moment push all they received at the seminar away into the background.

Write a report on the helpful information you have received relative to your own work and your own situation. Start with yourself and your own work. A written report will put in solid memorable form what you have received, and it is a good way to relate the information, or relay the information from the shelf to other people.

Having worked out an organizational chart, do not expect to push the ideas you have learned and believe to be useful up your chart. It will not work. Begin where you are. Then educate in other directions first, that is, down and sideways. There may even be the desire to change the constitution of your organization. Don't! Start applying the management principles in the organization as it is.

What Not to Do

1. Do not assume that you know everything about management.
2. Do not assume that management is a substitute for prayer or the fullness of the Holy Spirit.
3. Do not go to the organization and tell them how much they need to adopt these principles.
4. Do not expect to push these ideas up your organizational chart.
5. Do not try to change the constitution of your organization.

What to Do

1. Start within two weeks after reading this book, and start with yourself.
2. Write a report to your boss.
3. Begin to educate in four directions: down, sideways, and finally up.
4. Set aside some time to study management further.
5. Start a file of management information.

Bibliography

Alexander, John W. *Managing Our Work.* (Downers Grove, Ill.: Inter-Varsity Press. 1972. 84 pages, illustrated, bibliography.)
Deals with work management in the areas of planning, execution, review, continuing and growth management.

Appley, Lawrence A. *Formula For Success—A Core Concept of Management.* (New York: American Management Association. 1974, 138 pages.)
Deals with the problems that confront executives. The basic concept is that a manager must get things done through others by leading a group toward the attainment of common goals.

Batten, Joe D. *Tough-Minded Management.* (New York: American Management Ass'n. 1969. 218 pages, index.)
Shows how the manager tackles his duties of planning, delegating, and controlling. Discusses methods used to get things done through people, how to introduce change when necessary, the kind of people with whom a manager surrounds himself or herself.

Bruce, A. B. *The Training of the Twelve.* (Grand Rapids: Kregel Publishers. 1971. 552 pages, index. Reprint.)
Written about the turn of the century by the great Glasgow theologian treating thoroughly the Lord Jesus Christ and his work with his apostles.

Butt, Howard. *The Velvet Covered Brick—Christian Leadership in an Age of Rebellion.* (New York: Harper & Row. 1973. 186 pages, notes.)
This book takes unfashionable words—authority and submission—and dares to suggest their relevance today. It is deeply Christian and personal in tone; yet even "like-minded souls" will find it refreshing and full of surprises.

Classen, Willard. *Learning to Lead.* (Scotdale, Penna. Herald Press. 1963. 112 pages.)
Discusses the characteristics of immature and mature groups, communication, decision making, goal setting, and evaluation.

———. *Learn to Lead – Leader's Guide.* (to be used with above textbook.)

Coleman, Robert E. *The Master Plan of Evangelism.* (New York: 1978. Fleming H. Revell.)
A popular study of the relationship of Jesus and the Twelve. Written by the professor of Evangelism at Asbury Seminary. A must book!

Dayton, Edward R. *God's Purpose/Man's Plans.* (Monrovia, Calif.: MARC. 1971. A workbook.)
A logic diagramming technique called PERT is described as a useful planning tool. It discusses planning and goal setting as a response to God's purpose for the church and individual Christians.

Drucker, Peter F. *The Effective Executive.* (London: Heinemann, also New York: Harper & Row. 1966. 148 pages, index.)
Drucker identifies five "talents," knitting them together by effective decision making. How to develop these talents forms the main body of the book.

Gangel, Kenneth O. *Competent to Lead.* (Chicago: Moody Press. 1974. 144 pages, illustrated, bibliography.)
Dr. Gangel has touched the very nerve center of the work of the local church. He has grappled realistically, practically, and exceedingly helpfully with the issues that confront every leader in Christian work. A must!

Grossman, Lee. *The Change Agent.* (New York: American Management Ass'n. 1974. 168 pages.)
Gives pointers on how to make meaningful changes happen that are right for individuals and organizations.

Hodges, Melvin L. *Grow Toward Leadership.* (Chicago: Moody Press. 1969. Revised edition. 63 pages.)
This book focuses mainly on the area of spiritual leadership. The author cites examples and principles of executive responsibility as found in the Word of God.

Kepner, Charles H. and Tregoe, Benjamin B. *The Rational Manager—A Systematic Approach to Problem Solving and Decision Making.* (New York: McGraw-Hill. 1965. 275 pages, illustrated, bibliography, index.)
The authors have developed clear concepts and procedures that enable a manager to approach every problem systematically and to solve it efficiently. This is a practical, not a theoretical, book.

Kolivosky, Michael E. and Taylor, Laurence J. *Why Do You See It That Way?* (Hillsdale, Mich.: Hillsdale College. 1972. 2nd printing. 147 pages, illustrated.)
Contains principles of perception: most applicable principles for guidelines in inter-personal relationships. An excellent book!

Koontz, Harold and O'Donnell, Cyril. *Principles of Management—An Analysis of Managerial Functions.* (New York: McGraw-Hill. 1972. 5th edition, 748 pages, illustrated, case incidents, references.)
Furnishes a framework of basic knowledge organized and presented under the functions of planning, organizing, staffing, directing and controlling.

Laird, Donald A. and Laird, Eleanor C. *The Techniques of Delegating.* (New York: McGraw-Hill. 1957.)
The classic and best ever written on delegation. Don't let the date fool you. It is as current as can be as to strategy and principles.

Mackenzie, R. Alec. *The Time Trap.* (New York: American Management Ass'n. 1972. 195 pages, illustrated, notes, index.)
The author has packed this book with practical easy-to-apply tips that you can use to make yourself many times more productive than you ever thought possible.

Mager, Robert F. *Goal Analysis.* (Belmont, Calif.: Fearon Publishers. 1972. 136 pages, illustrated, selected references.)
Helps in answering questions like: What do you do about the affective domain? Why don't they have the right attitude? How can I motivate them? How can I deepen their appreciation?

Nichols, Sue. *Words on Target.* (New York: McGraw-Hill. 1957. 235 pages, bibliography, index.)
A valuable primer for anyone who wants to write and speak effectively. One of the best on this subject!

Odeirne, George S. *Management by Objectives.* (New York: Pitman. 1965.)
An old one, but a good one. Management by objectives starts here.

Rogers, Everett M. and Shoemaker, F. Floyd. *Communication of Innovations—A Cross-Cultural Approach.* (New York: The Free Press. 1971. Second edition, 476 pages, illustrated, bibliography, index.)
Integrates diffusion research with the scientific study of human communication; stresses communication concepts and frameworks in our analysis of the diffusion process.

Schaller, Lyle E. *The Change Agent.* (New York: Abingdon Press. 1972. 207 pages, notes, index.)
Deals concisely with identifying change, planning for change, anticipating and managing conflict caused by change, and so on. An excellent book!

Stone, W. Clement. *The Success System That Never Fails.* (Englewood Cliffs, N. J.: Prentice Hall. 1962. 252 pages, illustrated, bibliography, index.)
Shows how to do twice as much in half the time, how temporary failures can become permanent success, how to have the courage to enter the unknown...and much, much more.